Mark Ibbotson

Bryan Stephens

Business
START-UP 2

Student's Book

CAMBRIDGE
UNIVERSITY PRESS

CAMBRIDGE UNIVERSITY PRESS
Cambridge, New York, Melbourne, Madrid, Cape Town,
Singapore, São Paulo, Delhi, Tokyo, Mexico City

Cambridge University Press
The Edinburgh Building, Cambridge CB2 8RU, UK

www.cambridge.org
Information on this title: www.cambridge.org/9780521534697

First published 2006
10th printing 2011

Printed in Dubai by Oriental Press

A catalogue record for this publication is available from the British Library

ISBN 978-0-521-53469-7 Student's Book
ISBN 978-0-521-67208-5 Workbook with CD-ROM / Audio CD
ISBN 978-0-521-53470-3 Teacher's Book
ISBN 978-0-521-53471-0 Audio Cassettes (2)
ISBN 978-0-521-53472-7 Audio CDs (2)
ISBN 978-3-12-539768-2 Student's Book Klett Version

Contents

1 | Introductions

1 **a** **Talk about jobs.**

What's your job title in English?

Is your job common or very specialised?

Do you know anyone with a very unusual job?

b ▶▶ 1 **Ivan Magnusson, a trainer, is talking at the start of a training course. Listen and complete the information.**

1 Length of course: _____ days

2 Course name: International _____

_____

3 Ivan's job: _____ consultant

2 **a** ▶▶ 2 **Listen to Ella Grady, one of the people on the course, talking about her job. Fill in the gaps in the Organisation Chart.**

Organisation Chart

Sue Arpel
managing director

Responsibilities:
- 7 departments
- 145 people

David Kemp
customer service manager

Responsibilities:
- customer service department
- 3 regional customer service managers

Ella Grady
1 _____ *customer service manager*

Responsibilities:
- 2 _____ assistants
- 3 _____ countries

b **Which other person from the chart is on the training course?**

c **Fill in the gaps in these sentences from 2a.**

of after to with for

1 I look __*after*__ customer service for Europe.

2 I report _____ the customer service manager.

3 He's in charge _____ the department.

4 We're responsible _____ customers in Europe.

5 I deal _____ problems most of the time.

6

d ▶▶ **2** **Listen again and check your answers.**

e Vocabulary practice ···> Page 95, Exercise 1.

f **Work with a partner. Imagine you are one of the people on the chart. Describe your responsibilities. Use the language from 2c.**

g ▶▶ **3** PRONUNCIATION **Listen and repeat. How do these words change in sentences?**

1 **of** I'm in charge of the department.
2 **for** I'm responsible for customers.
3 **to** I report to the department manager.

> *Present simple:* **be**
>
> **I'm** an export manager.
> **He's** in charge.
> **We're** responsible for ten countries.
> **I'm not** in charge.
> She **isn't** on the course. (or She**'s not**)
> They **aren't** all here. (or They**'re not**)
>
> ···> Grammar reference 3.1.1

h **Fill in the gaps with these forms of the verb** *be.*

> are   is   I'm   he's   isn't   we're   they're   aren't   isn't

1 My name's Ella Grady. ___I'm___ in customer service. It _____ a very big department – only six people.
2 I'm not in charge of the department. David Kemp _____ the manager. _____ my boss.
3 I work with five colleagues. _____ in the European section of the department.
4 Alicia, Todd, Mike, Eric and Hans _____ all in my team. _____ my assistants.
5 Sue Arpel _____ on the course. There _____ any directors on the course.

3 **a** ▶▶ **4** **Listen to Ivan Magnusson telling the group about his 'secret job'. Then complete the sentences.**

1 Ivan works for _____ .
2 He writes reports about _____ .
3 The company doesn't pay him, but _____ .
4 Ivan is the right person for the job because _____ .

b Underline **the correct verb forms in these sentences that Ivan and David say.**

1 I *work/works* for a hotel company.
2 We *check/checks* customer service.
3 I *write/writes* a report.
4 It *don't/doesn't* take long.
5 I *don't/doesn't* pay.
6 They *travel/travels* a lot.
7 I *don't/doesn't* like the paperwork.

c ▶▶ **4** **Listen again and check your answers.**

> *Present simple*
>
> I **work** in this office. He **works** with me. He **doesn't work** here. We **don't work** together.
> *The verb* have *is irregular:*
> I **have** an assistant.
> She **has** a new job.
> I **don't have** an assistant.
> She **doesn't have** a new job.
>
> ···> Grammar reference 3.1.2

d Grammar practice ···> Page 95, Exercise 2.

4 Communication practice 1. Student A ···> Page 78. Student B ···> Page 88.

5 **Talk to a partner about your job (or a job you would like to do). Talk about your responsibilities and give examples of things you do at work.**

> USEFUL LANGUAGE
>
> I'm the international sales manager.
> I'm responsible for exports.
> I report to the managing director. She's my boss.
> I manage a team of ten engineers.
> The factory manager deals with production problems.
> I'm in charge of this project.
> I'm in after-sales service. I look after customers.

1 a Look at the title of the web page. What is the page about?

b Read about the IAAPA trade fair and answer the questions in the FAQs (Frequently Asked Questions) window.

Intrafair

Your online guide to International Trade Fairs
What? When? Where?

International Association of Amusement Parks and Attractions (IAAPA) Conference and Trade Show

Trade fairs aren't usually fun. But that's not true at the IAAPA, a conference and trade show for the amusement park business. This year, there are about 1,300 companies at the IAAPA. The show, from November 15th–20th, is at the Georgia World Congress Center, Atlanta. It's only open to professionals. There are thousands of products on exhibition, some of them enormous – including rollercoasters. The site is huge: 60,000 square metres, with indoor and outdoor areas.

The Amusement Park Business – Facts and Figures

Amusement parks aren't just big places. They're also big business. In the United States, amusement parks have over 300 million visitors a year, and customers spend over $10 billion a year. And it's a global industry – nearly every country has amusement parks of some kind.

FAQs

1 What do the letters IAAPA stand for?
2 Where is the fair?
3 When does the show start?
4 How many companies are at the fair?
5 Is the fair open to the public?
6 Are there rollercoasters at the show?
7 Does the fair have an outdoor area?

Present simple: questions

be
Is the trade fair in Montreal?
Where **are** your offices?
Other verbs
When **does** the fair start?
Do they make computers?

···> Grammar reference 3.1.1 and 3.1.2

c Grammar practice ···> Page 95, Exercise 3.

d ▶▶ 5 Listen and repeat the questions in the grammar box.

e Work with a partner. Take it in turns to ask and answer questions.

A Where do you work?
B I work in Berlin.

What / do?   Where / work?   What company / work for?   What / your company do?

2 a One of the companies at the IAAPA is Vekoma. Read the text below, then answer questions 1–3.

For a lot of firms, global business is a rollercoaster. But for Vekoma, rollercoasters are a global business. The Dutch company is one of the world's top rollercoaster builders. It exports to customers worldwide.

1 What does the first sentence of the text mean?
2 What does Vekoma make?
3 Is it an international company?

Vekoma provides a full service

c 1 Engineers design the rollercoaster to meet the customer's needs.

☐ 2 The factories produce the parts. Vekoma manufactures parts at two plants, in the Netherlands and the Czech Republic.

☐ 3 The company delivers the parts to the customer's site.

☐ 4 Vekoma's engineers and technicians install the rollercoaster.

☐ 5 Vekoma offers after-sales service. It advises customers about maintenance and safety and supplies spare parts.

b Read about the service that Vekoma offers. Match the photos to the sentences from the text.

c Match the definitions 1–7 to the verbs a–g.

1 offer goods/services   a design
2 sell abroad   b supply
3 create/draw   c deliver
4 make   d manufacture
5 help/give information   e install
6 build/put in   f export
7 transport/send   g advise

d Vocabulary practice ···> Page 95, Exercise 4.

3 a ▷▷ 6 **A salesman from a company called Fun Farm is talking to a potential customer at a trade fair. Listen and answer the questions.**

1 What does Fun Farm manufacture?
2 What's the woman's job?
3 Where does Fun Farm make its products?

b ▷▷ 6 **Listen again. What does the salesman say about:**

1 customers around the world?
2 installation and after-sales service in Germany?

4 Communication practice 2. Student A ···> Page 78. Student B ···> Page 89.

5 Ask a partner about the products and services of a company he/she knows well.

USEFUL LANGUAGE

We design, manufacture, deliver and install the products.
Do you supply parts?
We advise customers about maintenance.
Where do you export your products?
We have customers in 30 countries.

TIME OUT

1.3 | Eating out

VOCABULARY Understanding a menu Ordering a meal

1 a Work with a partner. Talk about eating out.

What's your favourite restaurant? Why do you like it?

b Look at the top of the menu. Talk about the restaurant.

Do you think it's an expensive restaurant? Why/Why not?

What sort of customers do you think go to this restaurant?

a apple pie with fresh cream or ice cream

b roast chicken, beef or lamb, grilled steak

c tomato soup

d fried haddock or cod, grilled salmon

Simply Delicious

Simple dishes ✓
Good food ✓
Great value ✓
Great service ✓

Choosing your meal is as easy as ... 1 2 3

1	Starters	Start simply with one of our light and tasty starters ...
2	Main courses	Meat or fish + 2 side dishes. You choose. 3 choices, 300 combinations ...
3	Desserts	Summer is here with our cool desserts ...

c Look at the extracts from the menu on the right. Match the dishes (a–h) to the parts of a meal (1–5).

1 starters: _c_ _____

2 meat for the main course: _____

3 fish for the main course: _____

4 side dishes: _____

5 desserts: _____ _____ _____

d Vocabulary practice ···▸ Page 95, Exercise 5.

e PRONUNCIATION Where's the stress? Fill in the chart.

| broccoli carrot chicken dessert haddock potato |
| salad salmon vegetable strawberry tomato |

Oo	oO	Ooo	oOo
		broccoli	

f ▸▸ 7 Check your answers. Listen and repeat.

g Work with a partner. Take it in turns to point at a picture of food and ask what it is.

A What's this? / What are these?

B It's/They're ... .

h Talk to your partner about what you would like for lunch. Choose a starter, main course and dessert from the menu.

For the starter, I'd like ... .

10

b **Fill in the gaps in the extracts from the conversation.**

> anyone else   anything else   fine thanks   a table
> no thanks   the bill   the same   a starter

1 **Waiter** Everything OK?
   David Yes, _fine thanks_ . Excellent.
   Waiter Can I get you _____ to drink? Or to eat?
   David Nothing for me. I'm fine, thanks. Ivan?
   Ivan _____ . I'm full, thank you.
2 **David** I think it's time to get back, actually.
           Could we have _____ , please?
3 **Ivan** Hello. We have a reservation. The name's
           Magnusson. _____ for three.
4 **David** Just a coffee for me, please. Would
           _____ like coffee?
5 **Ella** To start, the tomato soup, please.
   David Yes, _____ for me, please.
           The tomato soup.
6 **Ivan** I don't want _____ , just a main
           course. Can I have steak, chips and peas, please?

c ▶▶ 8 **Listen again and check your answers.**

d **Vocabulary practice ⋯> Page 96, Exercise 6.**

3 **Communication practice 3 ⋯> Page 78. Work with a partner.**

> USEFUL LANGUAGE
>
> I have a reservation. A table for three.
> For the starter / main course could I have ..., please?
> The same for me, please.
> Would you like a dessert?
> Would you like anything else?
> I'm fine thanks.
> Could I have the bill, please?

e fruit salad

f chips, mashed potato, rice, mixed vegetables, leeks in cheese sauce

g mixed salad

h strawberries and cream

2 a ▶▶ 8 **Ivan Magnusson and some people on his course are having lunch at Simply Delicious. Listen to four conversations and match them to a–d. Write 1–4 in the boxes.**

a ☐ Arriving at the restaurant
b ☐ Ordering the first two courses
c ☐ Ordering the last course
d ☐ Asking to pay for the meal

11

2 | Teamwork

2.1 | Discussing work in progress

GRAMMAR Present continuous

VOCABULARY Projects

1 **Read the comments. Which do you agree and disagree with? Say why.**

1 'It's important to plan work in detail.'
2 'You can't manage a project without a schedule.'
3 'To be realistic, add 30% to the budget of most projects.'
4 'Progress reports don't help much. They're always out of date.'

2 **a** ▶▶ 9 **John Perry, a British architect, is working on a project abroad. Vanessa Wood, from *European Life* magazine, is interviewing him by phone. Listen and answer the questions.**

1 Which country is John working in?
  In ....
2 What's the project?
  A ....
3 What's the budget for the project?
  €............... .
4 How much of the work is John paying for?
  ....%.
5 How long is the schedule?
  .... months.

b **Make sentences from the conversation. Use the present continuous.**

1 where / work ?
  Where are you working? ....
2 I / stay / in one of the rooms .
  ....
3 you / not / pay .
  ....
4 this project / cost / a fortune !
  ....
5 I / manage / the project .
  ....
6 At the moment, we / work / on the bathrooms .
  ....

c **Look at the transcript on page 115 and check your answers.**

> *Present continuous*
>
> Where **are you** working at the moment?
> I**'m working** in Italy.
> **Is** Kathy **working** with you?
> She **isn't working** on this project.
> *or*
> She**'s not working** on this project.
>
> ···▶ Grammar reference 3.2

d Grammar practice ···▶ Page 96, Exercise 1.

e ▶▶ 10 PRONUNCIATION **Listen and repeat. How does the pronunciation of *are* change when we say it in sentences?**

1 Where are you working?
2 Are you managing the project?
3 What are they doing?

f **Work with a partner. Use these verbs to describe what the people at the top of page 13 are doing.**

| build   design   paint   decorate   install |

1 They're decorating a room.

3 **a** Look at the schedule for work on the hotel. When does each part of the project start and finish?

Schedule	March	April	May	June – open 15th
Building work				
Decorating				
Website				
Brochure				

b It's May 1st. John is writing to his partners to give an update on the project. Fill in the gaps in the emails.

> on budget
> on schedule
> behind schedule
> under budget
> ahead of schedule
> over budget

c Underline phrases in the emails that mean:

1 we're having problems
2 finish (the work)
3 we're behind schedule

d Vocabulary practice ⋯> Page 96, Exercise 2.

4 Communication practice 4. Student A ⋯> Page 78. Student B ⋯> Page 89.

5 Talk to a partner about a project or job you're working on at the moment. How's it going?

Richard and Kathy,

Exactly six weeks to go before we open! Here's a short progress report.

As you know, the building work is now complete – so that's ¹ *on schedule* . However, we're having trouble with the interior designer and the decorating is starting late – 7th May. That means we're a week ² _____ . I still think we can complete the work before 15th June though.

How are things with you?

John

Hi John,

Thanks for the update. Good news here – the website is now ready two weeks ³ _____ . People can now book rooms online.

We're running late with the brochure though. And the paper that we want is quite expensive – which means we're a little ⁴ _____ . However, because of the lower cost of the website (it was £1,200 ⁵ _____) the whole project is still ⁶ _____ .

Speak soon,

Richard

USEFUL LANGUAGE

We can complete the job on schedule and on budget.
We're ahead of schedule and under budget.
We're having trouble/problems with one of the installations.
We're behind schedule. We're running two weeks late.
Costs are higher than planned. We're $25,000 over budget.

1 a Work with a partner. Match the descriptions of people (1–10) to the skills and characteristics (a–j).

1. [f] She works well with other people.
2. [ ] He certainly knows the business, after 30 years.
3. [ ] She always does a lot of work.
4. [ ] He has some really good ideas.
5. [ ] Things are changing fast, but she's coping well.
6. [ ] She's an excellent manager.
7. [ ] He always completes work on time.
8. [ ] He's very good at making presentations.
9. [ ] There's a lot of stress, but she can deal with it.
10. [ ] He's good at looking at problems in detail.

a creative
b hard-working
c experienced
d a strong leader
e reliable
f a good team player
g adaptable
h can cope with pressure
i a confident communicator
j analytical

b PAF, an advertising agency, is looking for young employees for its creative department. Work with a partner. Which skills and characteristics from a–j do you think the people need?

They need to be … .

c ▶▶ 11 Judith Lehman, the managing director of PAF, and Rowan Evans, the human resources manager, are talking about the type of people they're looking for. Listen and make notes.

The new people need to be:

creative, ...
....
....
....

d Look at the transcript for 1c on page 115 and check your answers.

e ▶▶ **12** PRONUNCIATION Listen and repeat. <u>Underline</u> the stress in these words.

1 reliable
2 confident
3 experienced
4 analytical
5 adaptable
6 creative

f Vocabulary practice ···> Page 96, Exercise 3.

2 a ▶▶ **13** PAF also needs to find a new creative department manager. Judith Lehman and Rowan Evans are talking about Marco Stone, a possible candidate. Listen and answer the questions.

1 Where does Marco work?
2 What are his main strengths?
3 What's the problem with making him the manager?
4 Do you think Judith and Rowan agree about Marco?

b Fill in the gaps in these sentences from the conversation.

> make   making   manage   managing
> sell   selling   work   working

1 We want someone to *manage* the department.
2 We need a manager to .... the new strategy work.
3 But .... Marco the department manager's also a risk.
4 OK, he enjoys .... for the company ...
5 ... but that doesn't mean he's good at .... a team.
6 The manager has to .... the new strategy to the team.
7 We know Marco's a good salesman. He likes .... ideas.
8 They work *with* him at the moment. What happens if they have to .... *for* him?

c ▶▶ **13** Listen again and check your answers.

Gerund

He's **good at** solv**ing** problems.
I'm **not very good at** mak**ing** presentations.
They **like/enjoy** work**ing** here.
(gerund after verbs of like/dislike)
Manag**ing** a big department isn't easy.

···> **Grammar reference 1**

d Grammar practice ···> Page 96, Exercise 4.

e What skills and characteristics do people need for these jobs? Give your opinion.

They need to be / be good at ... .
They need to like/enjoy ... .

- engineers   • salespeople
- fashion designers   • politicians
- chief executives

3 Communication practice 5 ···> Page 79. Work with a partner.

4 Talk about the skills and characteristics you need in your job or a job you would like to have.

USEFUL LANGUAGE

He's very experienced – 12 years in marketing.

Everyone likes working with him. He's a good team player.

We need a strong leader to manage the team.

He often works until late. He's very hard-working.

She isn't normally late. She's usually very reliable.

To make good presentations you need to be a confident communicator.

We're looking for creative people for the design department.

He's not good at solving problems because he isn't very analytical.

2.3 | Talking about your interests

VOCABULARY Sport and leisure   Likes and dislikes

Keywords (Google search)	Web pages (millions)
1	175.0
football	111.0
baseball	101.0
tennis	87.3
basketball	79.9
2	64.9
weight training	32.3
cycling	29.7
cricket	29.0
rugby	28.5
3	27.9
surfing	26.1
skiing	25.6
hiking	22.7
chess	17.4
boxing	16.8
horse riding	7.9
4	6.2
judo	4.6
ice skating	3.6
scuba diving	3.5
5	3.2
aerobics	2.8
elephant polo	0.3
6	0.2

1 **a** What are the most popular sports and leisure activities in your country?

b What do you think the most popular sports and leisure activities in the world are?

c The list on the right shows how many web pages you find when you search for sports and leisure activities with Google. Which activities can you see in the photos above? What do you think is number one on the list?

d Work with a partner. Can you complete the list with the six activities in the box?

> bowling   fishing   jogging   knitting
> golf   underwater hockey

e ▶▶ 14 Listen and check your answers.

f ▶▶ 14 PRONUNCIATION Which words in the list are the same or similar in your language? Is their pronunciation different in English? Listen again and check.

g Are any of the results on the list surprising? Do you think this is a reliable way to see which activities are the most popular?

2 a ▶▶ 15 Listen to two colleagues discussing their interests. Does the man like or dislike 1–3? Tick (✓) the boxes.

Man	☺	☹
1 Football	☐	☐
2 Golf	☐	☐
3 Horse riding	☐	☐

b ▶▶ 15 Listen again. This time, tick (✓) the boxes for the woman.

Woman	☺	☹
1 Football	☐	☐
2 Golf	☐	☐
3 Horse riding	☐	☐

c ▶▶ 15 Listen again and answer the questions.

1 Why doesn't the man watch football on TV?
2 Why does he talk about polo?
3 What's he interested in, apart from golf?

d Look at these sentences from the conversation. Match the pairs with a similar meaning. Write a–d in the boxes.

1 ☐ I can't stand it.
2 ☐ I can't play, that's my problem.
3 ☐ I'm not interested in it …
4 ☐ I'd love to have a go at riding …

a I'm hopeless at it!
b I bet it's good fun.
c I hate it.
d It's not my cup of tea.

e Vocabulary practice ⋯▸ Page 96, Exercise 5.

f ▶▶ 16 PRONUNCIATION Listen and repeat the sentences. <u>Underline</u> the word that's stressed.

1 It's <u>great</u> fun!
2 I'd love to have a go!
3 I hate it!
4 I can't stand it!
5 I'm hopeless at it!

3 Communication practice 6 ⋯▸ Page 80. Work with a partner.

4 Work with a partner. How many sports and activities can you remember from the Google search on page 16? Close your book and make a list. Then compare your list with the rest of the group.

> USEFUL LANGUAGE
>
> I enjoy playing golf.
> I can't stand football!
> I like watching ice skating.
> I'm hopeless at tennis!
> I'd love to have a go at surfing.
> I'm (not) interested in that.
> I really enjoy it. It's great fun!

3 Choices

1 **a** **Talk to a partner about online shopping.**

Do you sometimes buy things from Internet stores?
If so, what and why?

What products do people almost never buy online?
Why not?

What are the advantages and disadvantages of
shopping on the Internet?

b **Read the article. Then choose the best title
from a–c.**

a   **.comparison: why customers prefer
Internet stores to 'traditional' shops**

b   **.competition: why Internet stores
can't compete with 'traditional' shops**

c   **.combination: why customers want
Internet stores *and* 'traditional' shops**

c **Fill in 1–8 with words from the text.**

1   the cost of transport = *delivery charges*

2   not an extra cost = ... in the price

3   spend less = ... money

4   how good a product is = the .... of a
product

5   to order = to .... an order

6   money off the full price = a ....

7   products = ...

d **Read the article again. Are these sentences true
(T) or false (F)?**

1   Goods from shops often cost more
than goods from online stores.   ☐ T

2   At online stores, customers can try
on and feel the quality of clothes.   ☐

3   People often place orders at online
stores after looking at products in shops.   ☐

It's hard to talk about Internet shopping without
saying 'Amazon'. The company isn't just one of the
first online stores. It's also a good example of the
advantages of shopping online: finding and buying books
on a website is faster and easier than walking around a
shop. And because warehouses are less expensive than
shops, the company can offer lower prices even when
delivery charges are included. Customers save money.
And time. It doesn't get much better than that.

Clearly, a lot of products are not as easy as books to
sell online. People like to try on and feel the quality
of clothes when they choose them, for example. They
also like to look carefully at more expensive products.
This means going to a shop. And, of course, people
like shopping. But for online stores, these problems
are not as big as they seem. Today, people often look
at products in shops, then place an order at an online
store – at a discount.

If 'traditional' shops help Internet stores, the Internet
also helps traditional shoppers. The web is a good
place to find technical information about a product,
get a price and compare offers. But a lot of people
prefer not to buy more expensive goods online – they
do their research on the Internet, then go to a shop.

4   Compared with online stores, a lot of
shops offer bigger discounts.   ☐

5   A lot of people use the Internet
to compare products and quotes.   ☐

e **Vocabulary practice ⋯› Page 97, Exercise 1.**

2 a Find comparative forms in the text to complete 1–5.

1 quicker than = *faster* than
2 cheaper than = _____ _____ than
3 a lot better = _____ better
4 more difficult than = not _____ _____ _____
5 smaller than = not _____ _____ _____

Comparatives

Short adjectives
It's often fast**er** and cheap**er** to buy online.

Long adjectives
(+) BMWs are a lot **more** expensive **than** Skodas.
(–) Skodas are a lot **less** expensive **than** BMWs.

Irregular adjectives
The situation is **worse/better** now.

as ... as
This one isn't **as** popular **as** the other one.

···> **Grammar reference 2.1**

---

b Grammar practice ···> Page 97, Exercise 2.

3 a Vacscape.com is an online store which sells vacuum cleaners. The company has two quotes from suppliers. Work with a partner. Compare the vacuum cleaners, using these adjectives.

● cheap ● expensive ● old-fashioned ● modern

The Gravitas is cheaper than the Aerosaurus.

Supplier	**Gild**
Product	*Gravitas*
Price per unit	$240
50 units	$12,000
– 5% discount	$600
+ Cost of delivery	$2,500
Total cost	$13,900
Delivery time	15 working days

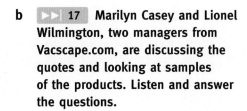

Supplier	**Suntra**
Product	*Aerosaurus*
Price per unit	$300
50 units	$15,000
– 12% discount	$1,800
+ Cost of delivery	$1,500
Total cost	$14,700
Delivery time	10 working days

b ▶▶ **17 Marilyn Casey and Lionel Wilmington, two managers from Vacscape.com, are discussing the quotes and looking at samples of the products. Listen and answer the questions.**

1 Is there much difference between the quality of the products?
2 What's the main difference between the products?
3 What does Marilyn think of the Aerosaurus?
4 What does Lionel think of the Aerosaurus?

c ▶▶ **18 PRONUNCIATION Listen and repeat. How do these words change in sentences?**

1 **than** It's cheaper than the other.
2 **as** It's not as cheap as the other.

4 Communication practice 7 ···>
Page 80. Work with a partner.

5 Work with a partner. Compare the price and quality of pairs of competing products and stores you both know.

● mobile phones
● supermarkets
● clothes shops

... is much cheaper, but the quality isn't as good ... .

... sells better quality products than ... .

USEFUL LANGUAGE

This product is better quality than that one.

The other quote is much cheaper.

Is there an extra charge or is the cost of delivery included?

If you place an order now we can offer you a five percent discount.

---

1 a What do you think of your company's offices? What do you like about them? What don't you like?

b Work with a partner. Discuss the opinions. Do you agree or disagree with them?

1 'Offices are just places to work. They only need to be basic.'

2 'Good offices and good facilities attract good people.'

2 a Look at the photos of three offices. Can you match them to the companies (1–3)? Write a–c in the boxes.

1 ☐ **Pixar**, the movie animation company based in California.

2 ☐ **McLaren**, the Grand Prix motor racing team, based in the UK.

3 ☐ **Wernham Hogg**, the company in the BBC TV comedy, *The Office*.

b Which of the three offices would you most/least like to work in? Say why.

c What's your opinion? Match the descriptions 1–10 to the offices in the photos. Write a, b or c in the boxes.

1 ☐ the oldest
2 ☐ the nicest
3 ☐ the most modern
4 ☐ the most horrible
5 ☐ the most unusual

6 ☐ the most original
7 ☐ the least expensive
8 ☐ the worst
9 ☐ the least advanced
10 ☐ the best

a

b

c

> **Superlatives**
>
> | (+) small | This is **the** small**est** office. |
> | (+) expensive | This is the **most expensive**. |
> | (–) expensive | That's the **least expensive**. |
> | (+) good/bad | I think this is **the best** and that's **the worst**. |
>
> ···> **Grammar reference 2.2**

d Grammar practice ···> Page 97, Exercise 3.

e **Work with a partner. Ask and answer the questions. Use the superlatives of the words in brackets.**

A What do you think is the best job in the world?

B I think ... .

1 What do you think is *(+ good)* job in the world?

2 What do you think is *(+ bad)* job in the world?

3 Which companies use *(+ advanced)* technology?

4 What's *(+ expensive)* restaurant in your town/city?

5 What's the *(+ unusual)* office building you know?

3 **a** **Work with a partner. Make a list of the equipment and rooms/areas people need in offices.**

Equipment	Rooms/Areas
photocopier	*meeting room*

b ▶▶ **19** **Listen to Steve Simpson, an architect, talking about the requirements for designing offices. Tick (✓) the things on your list in 3a that he talks about. Make a note of any other things he says.**

c ▶▶ **19** **Listen again. Are these sentences true (T) or false (F)?**

1 A coffee machine is an optional extra. ☐

2 It's important to have lots of light. ☐

3 Open plan offices are more expensive. ☐

d **Fill in the gaps in these sentences from the conversation.**

> | compulsory | difficult | essential |
> |---|---|---|
> | necessary | possible | important |

1 ... how much space do you need? And that's one of the most *difficult* questions.

2 So you want big windows, if
   ....

3 ... the most .... question is money. You know, cost is always the biggest problem.

4 ... walls cost money. If they're not an .... requirement, then why have them?

5 With anything that costs money, clients always ask, is it really
   .... ?

6 Offices are expensive, even if you only have what's in the regulations – what's ....

e ▶▶ **20** **Listen and check your answers.**

f Vocabulary practice ···> Page 97, Exercise 4.

4 Communication practice 8 ···> Page 80. Work with a partner.

5 **You're designing a new workplace for your partner. Discuss any problems with his/her present office and ask what your partner needs for the new office. Change roles.**

> **USEFUL LANGUAGE**
>
> The biggest/worst problem is space.
>
> The location is the most difficult question.
>
> We need a big meeting room – that's essential.
>
> I don't think fax machines are necessary any more.
>
> I'd like an extra table in my office, if possible.
>
> You need fire doors at the top of the stairs. They're compulsory.
>
> The most important question is cost.

1 Where would you like to have a holiday home? In your country? What about abroad?

2 a Read the first paragraph of the article. What sort of company is Vladi Private Islands?

b Read the rest of the article and fill in the gaps.

| tropical | lake | islands | coast |
| climates | forests | beaches | ocean |

ISLANDS FOR SALE
BUYING YOUR OWN PIECE OF PARADISE

Lots of people own, or would like to own, a holiday home in the sun. But imagine buying a whole island. It sounds like a dream, but for some people, private islands are a reality. There are hundreds of private islands around the world. Vladi Private Islands, an island real-estate agency, has nearly 100 properties for sale. And you don't have to be a millionaire to buy one – although it helps.

Some of the most beautiful properties are in the tropical regions of the Atlantic – in the Caribbean and the Bahamas. In the southern hemisphere, there are a few private [1] *islands* in French Polynesia, in the Pacific. There are also some places in the Indian [2] _____, mostly in the Seychelles, 600 km off the eastern [3] _____ of Africa. (Although, further east, there are thousands of islands around Indonesia, Malaysia, Thailand and the Philippines, there are almost no private islands in Asia.)

Typical prices for [4] _____ islands are between one and five million dollars. But if you don't have a multi-million-dollar budget, you can buy an island for as little as $100,000. However, instead of warm, white sand, you get cold, white snow, and an island on an icy [5] _____ in western Canada. Of course, mountains and pine [6] _____ can be as beautiful as [7] _____ and palm trees. In fact, some of the most expensive islands in the world are in colder [8] _____ – mostly in North America and Europe – not too far from the northern business capitals of New York and London, where their owners work.

c Where would you like to have a private island? Discuss with a partner.

d Work with a partner. Describe places in your country or abroad, and say where they are. Your partner tries to guess the name of the place. Take it in turns.

These are mountains in northern/southern ... not too far from ... .

It's a country/region in western/eastern ... with beautiful ... .

e ▶▶ **21** **PRONUNCIATION** Listen and repeat the names of places from the article. Do any of the places have similar names in your language? If so, is their pronunciation different in English?

the Atlantic   the Pacific   Africa   Europe
North America   Asia   Indonesia   Malaysia
the Philippines   the Bahamas

3 **a** ▶▶ **22** **Alistair Alby, from New Zealand, is on a business trip in Hawaii. He's having lunch with Caroline Carmen, a colleague. Listen and answer the questions.**

1 What does Alistair like about Hawaii?

2 What time of year is it in New Zealand?

3 Why does Alistair talk about Christmas dinner?

4 What's the name of the mountains he talks about?

5 What does he say about travelling on the South Island?

b Match the questions and answers from the conversation. Write a–e in the boxes.

1 [c] What's the best time of year to visit?

2 [ ] And what's the weather like?

3 [ ] So, what are the best places to see?

4 [ ] Do you need a car to travel round?

5 [ ] So, can you recommend some campsites?

a Pretty hot, usually.

b Yeah, I can give you some good addresses.

c Early summer's nice.

d Yeah. Or you can rent a camper van.

e The nicest part of the country's the South Island ...

c ▶▶ **22** **Listen again and check your answers.**

d ▶▶ **23** **PRONUNCIATION** **Listen and repeat. How do these words change in the sentences?**

1 **to**   Where are the best places to go?

2 **of**   What's the best time of year to visit?

3 **can** Can you recommend some campsites?

e Vocabulary practice ···> Page 97, Exercise 5.

4 Communication practice 9 ···> Page 80. Work with a partner.

5 Work with a partner. Talk about a tourist destination, in your country or abroad, that you would like to visit and say why.

> **USEFUL LANGUAGE**
>
> What's it like there?
> It's beautiful. The beaches are really nice.
> It's in the Pacific. It's on southern coast of ... .
> It's in the mountains, but it's not too far from the sea.
> What's the weather like in summer?
> What's the best time of year to visit?
> Can you recommend any good places to stay?

4 Experience

1 **a** **Discuss this sentence. Do you agree?**

'The simplest inventions are the best.'

b **Work with a partner. Why was the bicycle a successful invention? Describe its advantages.**

Bikes are … .

c ▶▶ **24** **Listen to Rob Martel, a marketing consultant, giving a training course about designing hi-tech products. Why does Rob use the bicycle as an example in his talk?**

d **Complete these sentences from the discussion.**

complicated dangerous low much often successful

1 I want to talk about the bicycle – a very *successful* invention.

2 They don't cost ....

3 A They're not ....
   B They're easy to use, yeah.

4 Running costs are ....

5 They don't .... break down.

6 They're not too ....

e ▶▶ **24** **Listen again and check your answers.**

f ▶▶ **25** **Listen to Rob summing up why the bicycle is so popular. Which adjectives does he use?**

1 *cheap*   4 ....

2 ....   5 ....

3 ....   6 ....

g **Vocabulary practice ···▶ Page 97, Exercise 1.**

2

a Look at the photo of the Sinclair C5. What do you think it is?

b Read the text. Was the C5 a success?

c Fill in the gaps with *was, were, wasn't* or *weren't*.

1 The Sinclair C5 _____ smaller than a car.

2 The C5 _____ very fast.

3 There _____ no seats for passengers in the C5.

4 The batteries in C5s _____ very big.

---

be: *past simple*

Was the product successful?
No, it **wasn't**. It **was** a flop.
Were the products successful?
No, they **weren't**. Sales **were** very low.

···❯ Grammar reference 4.1.1

---

d Grammar practice ···❯ Page 98, Exercise 2.

e Work with a partner. Take it in turns to ask and answer questions about the Sinclair C5.

A What was the C5?
B It was an electric vehicle.

What ... C5?   How big ...?   How fast ...?
... battery big?   ... advantages?   ... successful?

f <u>Underline</u> the correct words.

1 The Sinclair C5 *was/wasn't* big enough for one person.

2 The C5 was too *big/small* to carry passengers.

3 The battery *was/wasn't* powerful enough for long trips.

4 In the end, the market for the C5 was too *small/large*.

5 There was too *much/little* demand for the C5.

---

too/enough

The battery was **too small**.
The battery was**n't big enough**.

···❯ Grammar reference 2.3

The Sinclair C5 was a small electric vehicle with a top speed of 25 kph. The battery was big enough for trips of 10–20 km, and there were pedals, just in case there wasn't enough power to get you home. The idea for the C5 was based on a simple fact: most car trips are just a few kilometres, with only one person in the vehicle. In other words, cars are too big for their main use. The C5's small size and low cost weren't the only advantages: with electric power, pollution was zero. So why was the C5 such a flop? Was it too advanced for the consumers of 1985?

g Grammar practice ···❯ Page 98, Exercise 3.

h Work with a partner. Why do you think the Sinclair C5 was a flop?

i ▶▶ **26** Listen to Rob Martel discussing why the Sinclair C5 was a flop. Make a list of the reasons he gives.

3 Communication practice 10. Student A ···❯ Page 81. Student B ···❯ Page 89.

USEFUL LANGUAGE

It's not complicated. It's very simple to use.
The old products weren't reliable enough.
They were too dangerous. They weren't safe to use.
Was the product successful?
It was quite popular.
It doesn't use much electricity. It's very efficient and economical.

4.2 | Discussing past projects

GRAMMAR	Past simple: regular and irregular verbs
VOCABULARY	Problems and solutions

1 Talk about projects you worked on or jobs you did in the past. Which was:

- the most interesting/boring?
- the most difficult?

2 a Read the article about the BBC TV documentary, *Walking with Dinosaurs*. What were the three main problems on the project?

Problem 1: _____

Problem 2: _____

Problem 3: _____

b Work with a partner. Match the solutions a–c to the problems in 2a.

Problem 1 – Solution _____

Problem 2 – Solution _____

Problem 3 – Solution _____

(a) The only solution was to travel – a long way. The team went to California, Chile and New Zealand. It was expensive, and took a lot of time out of the two-year schedule, but it was the only way.

(b) The solution was to use moving models called 'animatronics'. With this technique, the camera could film a dinosaur's mouth, for example, as it ate or drank.

(c) Because the series was for TV, and not for the big cinema screen, the producers found they could use lower quality pictures than in *Jurassic Park*. So it was possible to use normal IT equipment, which made it less expensive.

In television, they say never work with animals. But what about filming dinosaurs? This was the challenge Tim Haines and his colleagues had when they made the BBC documentary series, *Walking with Dinosaurs*.

The team needed to solve some big problems before they could start work. The first was cost. *Jurassic Park*, the movie that gave Tim Haines his idea, cost over $60 million to make. The producers of the movie used very powerful, expensive computers to create the dinosaurs. The BBC also needed to use computers for most of the pictures, but couldn't spend as much as a big Hollywood film company. The budget for *Walking with Dinosaurs* was £6 million, a fraction of the cost of *Jurassic Park*.

c Complete the sentences. Use the past simple form of the verbs. Use the article to help you.

1 Tim Haines and his team ___*made*___ Walking with Dinosaurs. *(make)*

2 The BBC _____ a large budget for the series. *(not have)*

3 The series _____ £6 million and _____ two years to make. *(cost, take)*

4 Tim Haines _____ the dinosaurs to look as real as possible. *(want)*

5 The team _____ use computers to create all the pictures. *(can't)*

6 Researchers _____ locations in California, Chile and New Zealand. *(find)*

7 The team _____ all over the world to film. *(go)*

8 They filmed model dinosaurs as they _____ and _____ . *(eat, drink)*

9 They _____ computers for close-up pictures. *(not use)*

10 People all over the world _____ the series. *(watch)*

The second problem was the dinosaur's 'world'. It wasn't possible to use computers to create forests, lakes, mountains, etc. so the team needed to film at real locations. The trouble was, plants and rocks were very different at the time of the dinosaurs, so it was difficult to find realistic locations.

It was also impossible to use computers for dinosaurs that were near the camera. They just didn't look real. But Tim Haines wanted close-up pictures, so the people who watched the series could really 'walk with dinosaurs'. The team had to find a solution to this problem, so that all the pictures looked as real as possible.

Past simple: positive and negative

Positive
We start**ed** the project in February. (*regular*)
It **took** eleven months. (*irregular*)

Negative
The work **didn't take** long. We **didn't finish** on time.

···> Grammar reference 4.1.2 and 4.1.3

---

d Grammar practice ···> Page 98, Exercise 4.

3 a ▶▶ 27 **Jake Stern makes promotional videos for companies. He's talking to a customer about a video he made at a chemicals factory. Listen and answer the questions.**

1 What was the first problem Jake had?
2 What was the solution?
3 What was the second problem?
4 Was it possible to solve the problem?

---

b **Vocabulary practice ···> Page 98, Exercise 5.**

c ▶▶ 27 **Listen again and complete the questions from the conversation.**

1 **Jake**   Well, the trouble was, it was too hot for the camera.
   Client Oh, right. ¹_____ ?
   Jake   We put the camera in a box to protect it.

2 **Jake**   And we filmed with the camera in the box.
   Client And ²_____ ?
   Jake   Yeah, it worked OK.
   Client So how ³_____ the box? What ⁴_____ ?
   Jake   Just wood. Nothing complicated.

Past simple: questions

When **did** you **start** the project?
Did it **take** long?

···> Grammar reference 4.1.2

---

d **Grammar practice ···> Page 98, Exercise 6.**

e **Work with a partner. Take it in turns to ask and answer questions about *Walking with Dinosaurs*.**

How much ... cost?   Why ... need computers?
... have expensive computers?

What countries ... visit?   How long ... take?
How ... film close-up pictures?

4 **Communication practice 11. Student A ···> Page 81. Student B ···> Page 90.**

5 **Work with a partner. Take it in turns to talk about a project you worked on. What problems did you have? How did you solve them?**

USEFUL LANGUAGE

I worked on a difficult project last year.
We had problems/trouble with costs.
We needed to solve the problem quickly.
It was the only solution.
We couldn't do it. It was impossible.
It was possible, but it was very difficult.

4.3	Talking about the weekend	VOCABULARY	Life at home

Relaxing weekend?

1 a Read the sentences. Which one best describes you?

1 'I normally relax at weekends. After a hard week at work, I need a break.'

2 'I usually spend the weekend doing jobs I don't have time to do during the week!'

3 'I spend a lot of time with my family and visit friends.'

b Talk about these points. How do they change the amount of free time people have? Discuss any experiences you have, and give examples.

- age
- job
- where you live

2 a With a partner, look at the list of answers to the question, 'What did you do at the weekend?'. Match them to the pictures. Write a–j in the boxes.

1 [c] I cleaned the house.
2 [ ] I had a lie in.
3 [ ] I went shopping.
4 [ ] I watched TV.
5 [ ] I did some gardening.
6 [ ] I went to the cinema.
7 [ ] I cooked a big meal.
8 [ ] I did some work on the house.
9 [ ] I went out for a meal.
10 [ ] I had friends/family round.

b Can you guess what your partner did at the weekend? Tick (✓) the activities in 2a that you think he or she did. Then ask your partner to check your answers.

A Did you watch TV at the weekend?

B Yes. / No.

c Vocabulary practice ···> Page 98, Exercise 7.

d ▶▶ 28 Listen to a conversation between two colleagues. Tick (✓) the things that Dave did last weekend.

1 He sat in the garden. [✓]
2 He had some friends round. [ ]
3 He cooked a meal. [ ]
4 He did some gardening. [ ]
5 He worked on the house. [ ]
6 He had a lie in. [ ]

f Look at the transcript for 2d on page 117 and check your answers.

g Work with a partner. Ask and answer questions about Dave's weekend. Look at the transcript, if necessary.

What ...?   Where ...?   When ...?
What time ...?   Why ...?

3 ▶▶ **29** PRONUNCIATION Listen and repeat the questions. Copy the intonation.

1 Did you have a good weekend?

2 What film did you see?

3 Did you have a lie in?

4 Where did you go shopping?

4 Communication practice 12 ···▸
Page 82. Work with a partner.

5 Work in groups. Ask other students what they did last weekend. Talk about what you did.

e Complete the sentences from the conversation. Use the past simple form.

1 We ___ate___ outside yesterday, at lunchtime. *(eat)*

2 We _____ outside in the garden. *(sit)*

3 I _____ to buy some charcoal. *(forget)*

4 So you _____ in the sun ... . *(sleep)*

5 ... and your wife _____ all the cooking. *(do)*

6 I _____ quite a busy weekend. *(have)*

7 It was a bigger job than I _____ . *(think)*

8 I _____ up early on Saturday and worked all day. *(get)*

USEFUL LANGUAGE

Did you have a good weekend?
What did you do at the weekend?
I had a relaxing/busy weekend.
We had some friends round for dinner.
I cooked a big meal on Saturday night.
I had a lie in on Sunday morning.
I worked on the house all weekend.

5 | Arrangements

1 a **Which of these things do you often arrange?**

- meetings in your country/abroad
- visits to conferences
- visits to exhibitions
- video/telephone conferences

b **In international business, what are the advantages/disadvantages of making arrangements:**

- by telephone?
- by email?

2 a ▶▶ **30** **Michael Morgan and Sylvie Dam, are arranging a trip to a conference in San Francisco. Listen to their conversation and answer the questions.**

1 What do Sylvie and Michael decide to do?

2 What does Michael say he'll do today?

3 What does Sylvie say she'll do today?

4 When do they arrange to speak again?

b **Fill in the gaps to complete the expressions from the conversation.**

get	back	call	contact	give	look	speak	touch

1 phone someone = __*call*__ someone / _____ someone a call

2 talk to someone = _____ to someone

3 phone again later = phone _____ / _____ back to someone

4 phone or email someone = _____ someone / get in _____ with someone

5 find/check some information = _____ into something

c **Vocabulary practice ···> Page 99, Exercise 1.**

d ▶▶ **30** **Listen again and change 1–6 to make sentences from the conversation.**

1 I can look on the Internet after lunch.
   I'll *look on the Internet after lunch* .

2 Let me give her a call this afternoon.
   I'll _____ .

3 Why don't we catch the same flight?
   Shall _____ ?

4 Do you want me to look into flights to San Francisco?
   Shall _____ ?

5 If you want, I can contact the San Francisco office.
   Shall _____ ?

6 If you like, we can speak at about 4.30.
   Shall _____ ?

e **Look at the transcript for 2a on page 118. Check your answers.**

> **will/shall:** *offers and suggestions*
>
> *Offers:* **I'll ... . Shall I ...?**
> We need more information about this.
> **I'll** look on the Internet.
>
> We need to book our tickets.
> **Shall I** book them?
>
> *Suggestions:* **Shall we ...?**
> When can we talk?
> **Shall we** speak this afternoon?
>
> ···> **Grammar reference 8**

f Grammar practice ⋯> Page 99, Exercise 2.

g **Work with a partner. Student A reads sentences 1 and 3 and offers a solution. Student B reads sentences 1 and 4 and offers a solution. Change roles.**

Shall I ...? / I'll ... .

contact / get in touch / look into / call / get back to / find out

1 We can get there by train, but I'm not sure how long it takes.
2 I don't know what it costs, but my colleague has a price list.
3 I'll give you the address. I don't have it here, but it's in my office.
4 We need more information. Sylvie knows a lot about this.

3 ▶▶ **31** **PRONUNCIATION** Listen to four sentences. Which form of the verb do you hear? Tick (✓) the correct answer: a, b or c.

	a	b	c
1	I call ...	I'll call ...	I called ...
2	I talk ...	I'll talk ...	I talked ...
3	I email ...	I'll email ...	I emailed ...
4	I contact ...	I'll contact ...	I contacted ...

4 **Communication practice 13. Student A ⋯> Page 82. Student B ⋯> Page 90.**

5 **Work in groups of three. Plan a trip to a conference in San Francisco.**

You and your colleagues are attending a conference at the South San Francisco Conference Center on the 27th and 28th of next month. Use the information to decide what you need to do. Decide which jobs you'll do, which your colleague will do, and when you'll do each job.

A Shall I call the conference centre?
B OK, then I'll ... .
C Shall I ... ?

You need **tickets for the conference**. (You have the phone number and email address of the South San Francisco Conference Center.)

You need to book a **flight** from your country to San Francisco, and back.

- Where/How can you find information about flights?
- When will you fly there and back?
- How will you travel from your home to the airport?

You need to book **hotel rooms** in San Francisco.

- How many nights do you need to stay, and on which dates?
- Where will you stay? Are there any hotels near the conference centre?

USEFUL LANGUAGE

We need more information about this. Shall I look into it?
I'll get back to you next week.
I'll call/phone you this afternoon.
I'll contact / get in touch with Paula. I'll give her a call later.
I need to talk/speak to my colleague about this.

Spelling
cen**tre** (=UK) cen**ter** (=US)

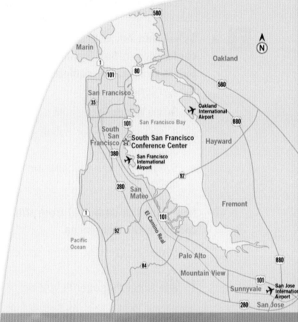

1 Do you agree with the following points?
What do you do?

1 'After a phone call I always make a note of what we discussed. If not, it's easy to forget things.'

2 'I normally send an email after a meeting to confirm the main points. It's good to have something in writing in case there's a disagreement or problem in the future.'

3 'In our company we send copies of decisions to all colleagues for information.'

2 a Sylvie and her colleague Michael are going to a conference in San Francisco. Read the email (a) from Sylvie to Rita, the conference organiser, and complete the sentences.

1 Sylvie sends Rita some _____ .

2 It isn't possible for Sylvie and Michael to meet

_____ .

3 Sylvie, Michael and Rita are meeting
on _____ .

b Now read the email (b) from the hotel to Sylvie and complete the sentences.

1 Earlier in the day, Sylvie spoke to

_____ .

2 The hotel manager is writing to confirm

_____ .

3 If Sylvie needs more information, she can

_____ .

c Work with a partner. Which of the emails (a or b) is formal and which is informal? Give examples of formal and informal words and phrases in the messages.

a

Hi Rita,

It was good to talk to you yesterday. Thanks again for helping me find a hotel.

Please find attached the slides for the presentation I'm making at the conference. It's a PowerPoint file – let me know if you can't read it, and I can send it as a Word document. Your comments will be welcome.

As discussed, my colleague, Michael Morgan, is coming with me to the conference. We're flying out on Wednesday, October 25th. Our flight gets into San Francisco at 11.00 pm, so unfortunately we can't meet you for dinner on Wednesday evening. But we look forward to seeing you on Thursday morning. The conference starts at 9.00, but I'll be there early to prepare for my presentation. It'll be a short night!

Bye for now.

Sylvie

b

Dear Ms Dam

Following our telephone conversation this morning, I confirm your hotel reservation for next month. Please find below details of the booking.

● 2 single rooms – in the names of Michael Morgan and Sylvie Dam, from Charing Medical Equipment

● 4 nights: October 25th to 28th inclusive

● Booking reference: 008956678 SR

As discussed, you're checking in after 23.00.

If you need any further details, please do not hesitate to contact me.

Best regards,

Luis Gomez,

Hotel manager.

d **Read the emails again. Find:**

1 two expressions to explain where
information is in the email:
Please find attached
....

2 two expressions to confirm an earlier
discussion:
....
....

3 one whole sentence to offer more
information/help.
....
....

e **Vocabulary practice ···> Page 99, Exercise 3.**

3 **a** **Look at these sentences. Do they describe
arrangements (A) or timetables? (T) Write A or T
in the boxes.**

1 We're checking in after 23.00. [A]
2 Our flight gets into San Francisco
at 11.00 pm. [ ]
3 My colleague is coming with me
to the conference. [ ]
4 I'm making a presentation at the
conference. [ ]
5 The conference starts on
October 26th. [ ]

> *Present tenses as future*
>
> *Future timetables/schedules: present
> simple*
> The flight lands at 11.00.
> *Future arrangements: present continuous*
> I'm flying to San Francisco next month.
>
> ···> **Grammar reference 5.1 and 5.2**

b **Grammar practice ···> Page 99, Exercise 4.**

4 **a** **▶▶ 32 Listen to Naomi Lind and Tom Dent
making arrangements for a meeting.
Complete the information.**

1 Date of meeting: ....
2 Time of meeting: ....
3 Document to email: the ....

b **Look at the transcript for 4a on page 118.
Check your answers.**

c **Now write an email, from Naomi Lind to Tom
Dent, to confirm the arrangements and send
the document as an attachment. Use these
words in your email.**

following   telephone conversation   confirm
attached   look forward to

> To: ...
> From: ...
> Subject: ...
>
> Dear Tom,
> ...

5 Communication practice 14. Student A ···>
Page 82. Student B ···> Page 90.

6 **Think of an email you wrote recently,
or emails you often write, to confirm
arrangements. Write the message in English.**

> USEFUL LANGUAGE
>
> I confirm the details of my flight below.
> My flight arrives at 11.00 pm.
> I'm coming to the conference with
> Michael Morgan.
> Please find attached the agenda for
> our meeting.
> As discussed, I'm arriving on Monday.
> Following our conversation, I attach
> the design.
> I look forward to seeing you next week.
> Please don't hesitate to contact me,
> if there's a problem.

1 a What do you know about:

- San Francisco?
- Alcatraz?

b Read the leaflet about Alcatraz and answer the questions.

1 When is Alcatraz open and closed?

2 What do you need to do if you want to visit Alcatraz in summer?

3 What's a 'shuttle'? Why is there one on the island?

4 What tourist information is available on the island?

5 What are the advantages of visiting Alcatraz in the evening?

c Now complete 1–8 with these words from the text.

> booklet guided history leaflet
> map museum peak periods
> souvenir tour

1 the busiest times = ...*peak*....

2 tourist information document = ... or ....

3 things that happened in the past = ...

4 a plan of a place, on paper = ...

5 something you buy to remind you of a place = ...

6 a place where visitors can see things from the past = ...

7 a visit with an expert who tells visitors about a place = ...

d ▶▶ 33 Check your answers. Listen and repeat.

e Vocabulary practice ⋯› Page 99, Exercise 5.

Sightseeing in San Francisco

Alcatraz

Alcatraz is San Francisco's most popular attraction. The jail, which closed in 1963, is open to tourists all year round, except Christmas Day and New Year's Day.

Getting there

You need to catch a ferry to get to Alcatraz Island. The trip takes just ten minutes. Ferries leave Fisherman's Wharf regularly, from 9.30 am to 6.30 pm in summer, and until 4.30 pm in winter. For trips during peak periods (summer and holidays), it's best to book before your visit, as tickets are often sold out a week in advance. See 'How to book' on the back page of this leaflet.

On 'the Rock'

When you get to 'the Rock', you're free to walk around the island and jail. Note that the short road from the dock (where all ferries arrive) goes up a hill. A shuttle service is available for visitors who can't walk up the road.

2 a ▶▶ **34** **Listen to four short conversations in a tourist information office in San Francisco. Match the missing words (a–d) to the beeps in the conversations.**

Conversation 1	**a**	maps
Conversation 2	**b**	leaflets
Conversation 3	**c**	souvenirs
Conversation 4	**d**	guided tour

b Fill in the gaps in these sentences from the conversations.

> anywhere   free   information
> opening   street

- Hello. Do you have any *information* about Alcatraz?
- Hi. Is there _____ near here where you can buy gifts and souvenirs?
- Can you visit the museum all day? What are the _____ times?
- Excuse me. Have you got any _____ maps?
- **A** How much are they?
  B They're _____ .

c ▶▶ **35** **Check your answers. Listen and repeat.**

3 Communication practice 15. Student A ⋯›
Page 82. Student B ⋯› Page 90.

4 **Work with a partner. Talk about tourism in your town/region.**

What are the most interesting places to visit?

What's available for tourists at the places (guided tours, souvenirs …)?

Further information

You can buy 'Self Guide' booklets (in English, Spanish, German, French, Italian and Japanese) at the dock on Alcatraz Island. These explain the history of the island and jail, and include a map. A shop near the dock sells other guide books and souvenirs. On arrival, visitors can also watch a video about Alcatraz and visit a small museum.

Alcatraz by night

It's possible to visit Alcatraz in the evening, on special guided tours. Visiting the island after dark offers some of the best views of San Francisco's city lights and the Golden Gate Bridge. See 'How to book', on the back page, for more information about tickets for evening tours.

USEFUL LANGUAGE

Excuse me? Is there a tourist information office near here?

Do you have any information/booklets/leaflets about the history of the island?

Do you have any maps of the city centre?

You can visit the museum with a guide. There's a guided tour every hour.

You can buy souvenirs from the museum shop.

For visits during peak periods, it's best to buy tickets in advance.

6 | Objectives

Permanent sunshine, uncertain forecast
Does Berlin's new Tropical Islands Resort have a bright future?

'The weather forecast's terrible. I think I'll go to the beach.'

It sounds like a strange idea. But in Brandenburg, just south of Berlin, you know it won't rain at the Tropical Islands Resort. The huge dome, which opened in March 2005, is larger than two football stadiums and higher than the Statue of Liberty. Inside, the temperature is 25°C. There's a 'sea' with water at 30°C, and even a small 'rainforest'.

Colin Au, the Malaysian businessman behind the project, thinks the resort will be successful thanks to the cold local climate and the dome's inland location. It'll certainly be more popular with Berliners than Germany's natural beaches, 250 km away. Especially in winter. However, with so many cheap flights to hot holiday destinations, it's hard to imagine large numbers of visitors coming from abroad. It'll probably be hard to attract tourists from western Germany, too.

If the resort is popular with local people, however, it's likely that more domes will open. After all, many of the world's big, rich cities have cold climates and, possibly, large markets for 'tropical daytrips'. But the Berlin resort won't really help to forecast the cost of domes in other places. That's because, from the start, the Brandenburg resort had a very big advantage.

1 **a** Look at the photos and talk about what you see.

b The Tropical Islands Resort is in Brandenburg near Berlin, in eastern Germany. Do you think that's a good location? Why/Why not?

c Read the article and answer the questions.

1 How big is the Tropical Islands Resort?
2 What's the climate like inside the dome?
3 What are the advantages of the location?
4 Why is there possibly a market for domes in other places?

d <u>Underline</u> the correct words to make sentences that match the points of view in the article.

1 The writer *thinks/doesn't think* a lot of visitors will come from other countries.
2 For the people of Berlin, the dome *will/won't* be more popular than Germany's coast.
3 The resort probably *will/won't* have a lot of visitors from western Germany.

> **will**: *predictions*
>
> I **think** the project **will** be successful.
>
> I **don't think** it'**ll** be very successful. (it'll = it will)
>
> Personally, I **think** it'**ll** / it **won't** be a success.
>
> ···> Grammar reference 5.4.1

e Grammar practice ···> Page 99, Exercise 1.

2 a ▶▶ **36** Listen to Caroline Flint, a tourist industry investment analyst, talking about this resort and the market for tropical domes. What was the Brandenburg resort's big advantage?

b ▶▶ **36** Listen again. Are these sentences true (T) or false (F)?

Caroline thinks:

1 the resort will possibly be successful in the long term. [T]

2 the number of visitors will probably be low in the first few months. [ ]

3 it definitely won't help to predict the success of other resorts. [ ]

4 the resort will certainly be popular with families. [ ]

5 perhaps somebody will build another dome, somewhere. [ ]

6 maybe there's a very large market for tropical domes. [ ]

c Correct the false sentences in 2b to match what Caroline said.

d Now fill in the chart with these words from 2b.

| certainly   maybe   probably |
| definitely   possibly   perhaps |

Very certain	Quite certain	Not certain
certainly		

e Which of the words in the chart in 2d go at the start of a sentence? Which go before the verb?

f Vocabulary practice ⋯> Page 100, Exercise 2.

g ▶▶ **37** PRONUNCIATION Listen to these sentences and underline the stressed words. How does the stress affect the pronunciation of *will*?

1 So, do you think the resort will be successful in the long term?

2 I think it'll probably be quite popular in the short-term.

3 I think a lot of people will probably come to have a look.

4 They'll want to see what it's like.

5 So the project will be good for getting information about the market.

h Work with a partner. Talk about tropical domes.

Do you think the Berlin resort will be successful in the long term?

Do you think companies will build domes in other locations?

3 Communication practice 16 ⋯> Page 83. Work with a partner.

4 Talk to a partner about a project you're planning or starting soon. Explain what you want to do, then make forecasts about the project.

How long do you think the project will take?

What difficulties/problems do you think you'll have?

> USEFUL LANGUAGE
>
> I think there'll probably be a lot of demand.
>
> Maybe/Perhaps the project will be successful.
>
> Do you think the resort will be popular?
>
> Possibly/Possibly not. It's difficult to say.
>
> I think it'll definitely/certainly be a success.

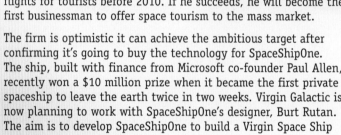

VIRGIN GOES GALACTIC

Sir Richard Branson, the boss of Virgin, is the type of person who believes the sky's the limit. But his next goal is to go one step further and do business in space. Branson's latest company, Virgin Galactic, is aiming to start space flights for tourists before 2010. If he succeeds, he will become the first businessman to offer space tourism to the mass market.

The firm is optimistic it can achieve the ambitious target after confirming it's going to buy the technology for SpaceShipOne. The ship, built with finance from Microsoft co-founder Paul Allen, recently won a $10 million prize when it became the first private spaceship to leave the earth twice in two weeks. Virgin Galactic is now planning to work with SpaceShipOne's designer, Burt Rutan. The aim is to develop SpaceShipOne to build a Virgin Space Ship

1

a Discuss these opinions about space tourism. Do you agree with any of them? Say why.

1 'Perhaps one day there'll be tourism in space, but certainly not in the next ten years.'

2 'I think space tourism will be a big industry, and it'll probably start in three or four years.'

3 'Maybe tourists will go into space in ten or twenty years, but only very, very rich tourists!'

b Read about Virgin Galactic. Tick (✓) the phrases that describe the company's objectives.

1 Take tourists into space. ✓
2 Produce a completely new design for a spaceship. ☐
3 Build a spaceship from current technology. ☐
4 Offer tickets cheap enough for most tourists. ☐
5 Take tourists for holidays in space. ☐
6 Allow passengers to float inside a spaceship. ☐

c Make sentences to describe Virgin Galactic's aims and objectives. Use the present continuous.

1 Virgin Galactic / plan / use the technology from SpaceShipOne.

Virgin Galactic is planning to use the technology from SpaceShipOne.

2 the company / aim / start space flights soon.

----

3 Virgin / hope / achieve its objective this decade.

----

4 the firm / go / build a ship called Virgin Space Ship.

----

d Work with a partner. Ask and answer questions about Virgin Galactic's plans.

A What are they planning to call the spaceship?
B They're planning to call it ... .

1 what / plan / call the space ship ?
2 what altitude / aim / reach ?
3 when / hope / start flights ?
4 who / go / work with ?

(VSS). A key objective will be to pass safety tests, which will allow VSS to carry paying passengers.

Space tourism is not a completely new business. In 2001, Dennis Tito paid $20 million for an eight-day trip to the International Space Station. Virgin Galactic is hoping to offer flights at much lower prices, possibly costing about $200,000 – not cheap, but a realistic sum for a growing number of rich tourists. To make this possible, the plan is to offer short trips to the limit of the atmosphere. VSS will spend just a few minutes at an altitude of about 350,000 feet (passenger planes fly at about 35,000). Passengers will be weightless, and have spectacular views of the earth and stars.

e **Find words in the text with similar meanings.**

1 a plan = a g_oal_ , a t................. ,
an a................. or an o.................

2 a plan that will be difficult to achieve =
an a................. plan or an o................. plan

3 a plan that will probably work =
a r................. plan

f Vocabulary practice ···> Page 100, Exercise 3.

2 **a** ▶▶ **38** **Listen to Caroline Flint, a tourist industry investment analyst, talking about space tourism. Circle the correct answer, a or b, to match her views.**

1 Space tourism in five years is ....
a realistic **b** optimistic

2 Ticket prices of $200,000 are a ....
a first target **b** final target

3 The priority for space tourism is ....
a good marketing **b** good safety

b **Match the pairs to make sentences from the conversation. Write a–d in the boxes.**

1 ☐ If a flight costs under $50,000,
2 ☐ If tickets cost over $500,000,
3 ☐ If it's too short,
4 ☐ If the first company is successful,

a very few people will buy them.
b a lot of others will follow.
c I think there'll be a lot of demand.
d then people won't be happy.

c **Look at the transcript for 2a on page 119 and check your answers.**

> ### First conditional
>
> **If** the project **is** successful, they**'ll** make a lot of money.
> There**'ll be** a lot of demand, **if** the price **is** reasonable.
>
> ···> **Grammar reference 6.1**

d Grammar practice ···> **Page 100, Exercise 4.**

3 Communication practice 17 ···> **Page 83. Work with a partner.**

4 **a** **Talk about Virgin Galactic's objectives. Do you think they're realistic?**

b **Work with a partner. Take it in turns to talk about a project that you're working on at the moment. What are your objectives? Are they realistic?**

USEFUL LANGUAGE

We're going to start a new company.
They're planning to develop the technology.
We're aiming to finish the project in December.
Our objective/aim/target/goal is to finish this year.
Do you think it's a realistic objective?
No, I think it's a bit optimistic/ambitious.
We're hoping the project will be successful.

1 a **Which are the most popular airlines in your country? Why are they popular?**

b **Look at the advert below for GlenAir, a low-cost airline.**

Do you have airlines like this in your country?

What are the disadvantages of very cheap plane tickets?

GlenAir ✈

Low-cost flights to Europe from Glasgow. Book your seat in advance for even lower fares.
Discounts for under 26s!

Rome **from £10**
one-way

Barcelona £40
return

Book now at **www.glenair.com**
or call 087100 – 432566

Prices do not include airport taxes. 20kg maximum baggage allowance on all flights. Excess baggage costs £6 per kilogram. Tickets are non-refundable and non-transferable.

c **Find words and phrases in the advert with the same meaning.**

1 If you buy your ticket early, you'll get a good price.
Book your seat in advance for even lower prices.

2 We don't pay money back and you can't change your ticket.
....

3 a single ticket
....

4 a ticket to go and come back
....

5 less expensive tickets
....

6 extra luggage
....

7 Young people pay less.
....

8 a limited amount of baggage
....

9 a long time before you travel
....

10 reserve
....

d **Vocabulary practice ···> Page 100, Exercise 5.**

2 a ▶▶ **39 Listen to a customer booking a flight with GlenAir. Answer the questions.**

1 Where does he want to go?
2 What type of ticket does he want?
3 What item of luggage does he want to take?

b ▶▶ **39 Listen again. Complete the information.**

1 Date of departure: _24th_ May
2 Date of return trip: .... May
3 Price of ticket: £..........
4 Baggage allowance: .... kg
5 Excess baggage charge: £.......... per kg

c Put the words in order. Make sentences from the conversation.

1 fly / to / end / Lisbon / at / the / like / to / of / May / I'd .
I'd like to fly to Lisbon at the end of May.

2 date / what / leave / planning / to / you / are ?

3 the / come / want / back / 31st / I / on / to .

4 cheapest / fare's / pounds / return / fifty-five / the .

5 extra / are / charges / there / any ?

6 baggage / maximum / the / what's / allowance ?

7 the / excess / is / pounds / charge / per / baggage / kilogram / six .

d Work with a partner. Student A plays the part of the airline assistant. Student B plays the part of the customer. Invent sentences. Change roles.

A Hello, can I help you?
B Yes. I'd like to fly to ... .

1 **Assistant** Hello, can I help you?
   Customer ....

2 **Customer** .... ?
   Assistant I'm sorry, the ticket is non-transferable.

3 **Assistant** The price is £150.
   Customer .... ?

4 **Assistant** OK, so you'd like a ticket to Madrid?
   Customer Yes. .... ?

5 **Customer** .... ?
   Assistant No, all taxes are included in the price.

6 **Assistant** When would you like to return?
   Customer ....

7 **Customer** .... ?
   Assistant 20kg.

3 a Now listen to the rest of the conversation. Can the customer choose his seat now?

b ▶▶ 40 Listen again and complete the details of the booking.

Flight GA66 Glasgow [Lisbon]
Passenger name
Payment method
Card number
Expiry date

Outbound flight – 6.50 ☐ or 14.30 ☐ (please tick)
Return flight – 17.30 ☐ or 22.00 ☐ (please tick)

c Work with a partner. Look at the transcript on page 119. Practise the dialogue with your own name. Invent a credit card number. Change roles.

4 Communication practice 18. Student A ⋯> Page 83. Student B ⋯> Page 91.

5 Work with a partner. Discuss air travel.
Which airlines do you use?
Which is your favourite airline?
Do you often fly long distances?
Do you like travelling by plane? Why/Why not?

USEFUL LANGUAGE

I'd like to book a flight to Barcelona.
If you book two months in advance there's a 10% discount.
Are there any extra charges or is everything included in the fare?
If I cancel the booking can I get a refund?
If you go over the baggage allowance, the excess baggage charge is €10 per kg.

7 | Success

1 a When did you start work at your present company? Compare with other people in the group.

b Work with a partner. Talk about the best times in your education and career. Why did you enjoy them?

2 a Look at this notice from PolyVec, a manufacturer of plastic products. What is it about?

Promotion of Jerome Gilder to Production Manager (Melbourne)

I am very pleased to announce that we have promoted Jerome Gilder to production manager at our Melbourne plant. Jerome will start work in his new position at the beginning of next month.

Jerome has worked at a number of PolyVec's branches. He joined the company in 2002, and spent some time as a production planner, first in our Boston office, then at head office in the UK. He then moved to South Africa three years ago, to work in his present position – assistant production manager at our Cape Town plant.

Jerome has worked for two other companies. He started his career with Alton, as a management trainee. He then left to join BTE, where he worked in production planning. Jerome studied Business and Economics at Cambridge University. He graduated in 1994, and spent the following year at the Sanford Institute of Technology, where he did a Masters in Distribution Management.

Congratulations to Jerome on his promotion. I'm sure he will continue to enjoy a successful career with PolyVec.

Simon Atkins, Production Director,
PolyVec International

b Work with a partner. Use the information in the notice to complete this part of Jerome's CV. Imagine the date on the notice is this month.

PolyVec
Assistant Production Manager (........–........)

PolyVec
Production Planner   (........–........)

BTE
Production Planner   **(1999–2002)**

Alton
Management Trainee   **(1996–1999)**

Sanford Institute of Technology
Masters   (........)

Cambridge University
Degree   **(1991–........)**

c Complete the sentences. Use verbs from the notice in 2a.

1 Jerome _studied_ Business and Economics.
2 He .... from Cambridge University.
3 He .... a Masters at SIT.
4 He .... Alton in 1996.
5 He .... Alton in 1999.
6 He .... his first years at PolyVec in the UK.
7 After working in the UK, he .... to South Africa.
8 Last week, PolyVec .... him to production manager.

d Vocabulary practice ···> Page 100, Exercise 1.

e Work with a partner. Ask and answer questions about Jerome's education and career. Use the past simple.

A When/Where/What did he ...?
B He ... .

Present perfect: negatives and questions

Have you us**ed** this software **before**?
Have you **ever** work**ed** with this software?
No, I **haven't** work**ed** with this.
I**'ve never** us**ed** it.

···> **Grammar reference 4.2.1 and 4.2.2**

c Grammar practice ···> Page 101, Exercise 3.

d ▶▶ **42** PRONUNCIATION **Look at the sentences. How do we say *have* in these sentences? Listen and repeat.**

1 Have you ever used this programme?
2 I've worked for several large companies.
3 I haven't worked with him before.

e **Work with a partner. Ask each other questions. If the answer is 'yes' then ask for more information.**

A Have you ever worked in a restaurant?
B Yes, I have.
A Where did you work?
B I worked in ... .

work / restaurant ?
live / foreign country ?
have / really bad job ?
work / difficult person ?

4 Communication practice 19. Student A ···> Page 84. Student B ···> Page 91.

5 **Work with a partner. Ask about his/her education and career.**

Have you (ever) ...?
Where / What / When did you ...?

USEFUL LANGUAGE

Which companies have you worked for?
Have you ever worked abroad?
What did you study at university?
Did you do a Masters?
I've worked for several large companies.
I left ZY Systems in 1994.
I joined my current company a year later.

Present perfect/Past simple

Present perfect
Jerome **has** work**ed** at a number of branches.

Past simple
Jerome join**ed** the company in 2002.

···> **Grammar reference 4.2.1 and 4.2.3**

f Grammar practice ···> Page 100, Exercise 2.

3 a ▶▶ **41** **Listen to a conversation between Jerome and his new assistant, Maria Doan, on his first day as production manager. Which of these computer programmes has Jerome used? Tick (✓) the boxes.**

1 Nurec ☐ 2 TP Control ☐
3 Arrow ☐ 4 Conductor ☐

b ▶▶ **41** **Listen again. Complete these extracts from the conversation.**

1 **Jerome** Nurec?
  Maria Yeah. _Have_ you worked with it before?
  Jerome No, I _____ used that one.
2 **Jerome** ... we used a system called Arrow.
  Maria Oh, _____ worked with that before.
3 **Maria** I know. And _____ changed so many times, as well. _____ you ever used Conductor?
  Jerome Conductor? No. I've _____ heard of it.

43

7.2 | Giving an update

GRAMMAR Present perfect: *yet / already / so far*

VOCABULARY Good news and bad news

---

1 **Underline words to make sentences that are true for you. Discuss the reasons for your answers.**

1 'In my job, it's *easy/hard* to plan work. It's *easy/hard* to know how long it will take.'

2 'Work *usually goes/doesn't usually go* to plan. It's *easy/hard* to work to a schedule.'

3 'The busiest time is usually at the *beginning/end* of a project.'

2 **a** **Read the email and answer the questions.**

1 What project is Andy Bell working on?

2 What parts of the project are going well?

3 What problems is Andy having?

b **Fill in the chart with the highlighted phrases 1–7 from the email.**

Good news
We've made good progress with ...
Bad news

c Vocabulary practice ···▸ Page 101, Exercise 4.

TO Yves Cordier **FROM** Andy Bell **SUBJECT** Progress report

Dear Yves,

Please find below a report on progress here at the new Singapore branch.

¹ We've made good progress with the new accounts department. I've already hired three accountants and I'm interviewing an accounts assistant next week. This means ² we're three weeks ahead of schedule with recruitment for that department. ³ Unfortunately, we're having problems with the IT installation. ⁴ We've had trouble finding IT people, so we haven't made much progress there. We've only found one technician so far (we need another two), and she hasn't started work yet – she's starting next Monday. That means ⁵ we're two weeks behind schedule with IT. I've written to Daniela in Zurich to ask her if she can send us someone from the office there. She hasn't replied yet. I'll give her a call today.

Our new sales rep ⁶ Anna is doing very well. So far, she's been to Bangkok, Manila, Jakarta, Hong Kong, and has just gone to Seoul. She's only been here four weeks and she's already flown to half of the cities in Asia! It certainly hasn't taken her long to make a start. She's sent me a few text messages to say her meetings have gone well. She's seen about 20 clients so far. And she's also done a big presentation at the FTO trade fair in Hong Kong.

So, in general, I think ⁷ things are going well. We can still open the office on schedule, if we can solve the problem with the IT people. I'll send another progress report next week.

Best regards,

Andy

---

3 **a** **What are the past participles of these irregular verbs? Look at the email again to help you.**

1 be ___*been*___   7 go _____

2 make _____   8 fly _____

3 find _____   9 take _____

4 have _____   10 send _____

5 write _____   11 see _____

6 do _____

b ▶▶ **43** **Listen and repeat. Then practise saying the verbs with a partner. Test each other.**

c Look at the sentences. What's the difference in meaning?

1 Anna has gone to Kuala Lumpur.
2 Anna has been to Kuala Lumpur.

4 a Look at Andy's 'to do' list. Use the information in the email to tick (✓) which jobs are completed.

To do:		
1	hire three accountants	✓
2	hire an accounts assistant	☐
3	find three IT technicians	☐
4	write to Daniela	☐
5	phone Daniela	☐

b Circle the correct sentence (a or b), based on Andy's 'to do' list in 4a.

1 **(a)** He's already hired three accountants.
  b He hasn't hired three accountants yet.
2 a He's already hired an accounts assistant.
  b He hasn't hired an accounts assistant yet.
3 a He's already found three IT technicians.
  b He's found one IT technician so far.
4 a He's already written to Daniela.
  b He hasn't written to Daniela yet.
5 a He's already phoned Daniela.
  b He hasn't phoned Daniela yet.

Present perfect: **yet/already/so far**

Have you written that report **yet**?
I've started it, but I haven't finished it **yet**.
We're doing well. We've **already** done most of the work.
I'm reading your report. I've read half of it **so far**.

···> Grammar reference 4.2.4

c Grammar practice ···> Page 101, Exercise 5.

5 a ▶▶ **44** Andy calls his boss, Yves, a week later to give another update. Listen to their conversation. Do you think Yves is happy with Andy's progress?

b ▶▶ **44** Listen again. Which jobs from Andy's 'to do' list in 4a are now completed?

c ▶▶ **45** PRONUNCIATION Listen and repeat the questions. Copy the intonation.

1 Have you opened the office yet?
2 Have you hired an accounts assistant yet?
3 Have they installed the IT system yet?

d Look at the 'to do' list of tasks for opening a new office. Ask your partner questions using *yet*. Answer with *yet*, *already* and *so far*. Change roles.

A Have you found an office yet?
B Yes, I have.

1	find an office	✓
2	hire staff:	
	sales and administration	✓
	accounts and IT personnel	X
3	install phones and Internet	X
4	write staff handbook	X
5	train staff	X
6	organise visit from head office	✓

6 Communication practice 20. Student A ···> Page 84. Student B ···> Page 91.

7 Write an email based on the update you gave in Exercise 6. Use the email on page 44 to help you.

USEFUL LANGUAGE

We're doing / We've done well.
Things are going / have gone well.
We're making / We've made good progress.
We aren't making / We haven't made much progress.
We're having / We've had problems with the installation.
We're having / We've had trouble with it.

1

a Look at the photos in the article. What do they tell you about Steve Fossett?

b What do you think the article is about?

c Fill in the gaps in the first paragraph of the article with the verbs.

been broken done driven flown
become ridden run swum won

d Have you ever done any of the things Steve Fossett has done? Is there anything you wouldn't like to do?

e Read the rest of the article. Use a dictionary to help you. According to the article, why does Steve Fossett do these types of activities?

2

a Look at the groups of adjectives. <u>Underline</u> the odd one out in each group.

1	amazing	fantastic	incredible	terrible
2	dangerous	frightening	relaxing	scary
3	bored	sad	interested	tired
4	difficult	happy	hard	tough

b Some adjectives have two forms, one ending *-ed*, the other *-ing*.

amazed/amazing   frightened/frightening
relaxed/relaxing   bored/boring
interested/interesting   tired/tiring

Which form describes feelings? Which form describes things or experiences? Give examples. Use the text to help you.

c Work with a partner. Imagine you did the things in the sentences 1–5. Talk about the experiences and your feelings.

It was ... / I was ... .

1 I walked up to the top of the Eiffel Tower.
2 Our flight was delayed for eight hours.
3 I spent the whole day just lying on the beach.
4 I did a parachute jump from 1,000 metres.
5 We spent the afternoon in the railway museum.

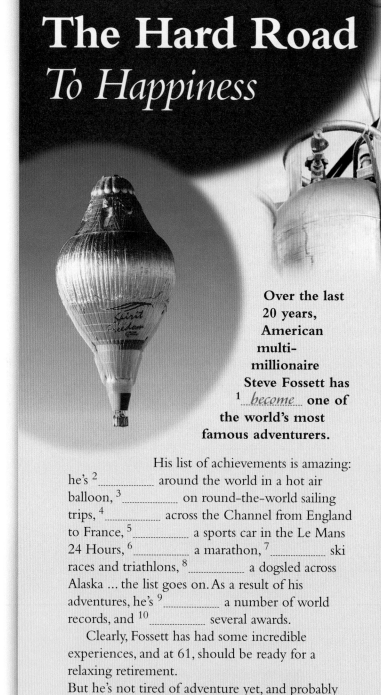

The Hard Road
To Happiness

Over the last 20 years, American multi-millionaire Steve Fossett has ¹ _become_ one of the world's most famous adventurers.

His list of achievements is amazing: he's ² _____ around the world in a hot air balloon, ³ _____ on round-the-world sailing trips, ⁴ _____ across the Channel from England to France, ⁵ _____ a sports car in the Le Mans 24 Hours, ⁶ _____ a marathon, ⁷ _____ ski races and triathlons, ⁸ _____ a dogsled across Alaska ... the list goes on. As a result of his adventures, he's ⁹ _____ a number of world records, and ¹⁰ _____ several awards.

Clearly, Fossett has had some incredible experiences, and at 61, should be ready for a relaxing retirement.

But he's not tired of adventure yet, and probably never will be. That's because he knows the key to happiness – something money can't buy.

According to psychologists, past success isn't enough. Even if their most fantastic dreams come true, most people are only happy for a short time, then they quickly return to 'sad' normality.

They then need another challenge, preferably more interesting, more fun or more frightening than the last one. In other words, if you've been on scary adventures before, you need to be scared again. And again. Steve Fossett has certainly made his life tough and dangerous. But it's much less terrible than the alternative: getting bored to death.

d Vocabulary practice ···> Page 101, Exercise 6.

3 **a** ▶▶ **46** **Listen to Lisa Grey and her colleague, Brendan Farmer, having a conversation. What subjects to they talk about? Why do they talk about them?**

b ▶▶ **47** **Now listen to the second part of the conversation. Are these sentences true (T) or false (F)?**

1 Lisa did a parachute jump last year. ☐ F
2 She enjoyed the experience. ☐
3 She was frightened before she jumped. ☐
4 After her parachute opened, she was scared. ☐
5 She had a very hard landing. ☐

c ▶▶ **47** **Listen again. Which adjectives does Lisa use to describe the experiences from 3b?**

d ▶▶ **48** **PRONUNCIATION With very positive or very negative adjectives, like *amazing* and *terrible*, we put extra stress on the word to give more emphasis. Listen and repeat. Copy the stress and intonation in the sentences.**

1 It was amazing!
2 It was incredible!
3 It was fantastic!
4 It was terrible!
5 It was awful!

4 Communication practice 21 ···> Page 84.
Work with a partner.

5 Tell other students about your most memorable or interesting experiences.

> ### USEFUL LANGUAGE
>
> Have you ever driven a sports car?
> Yes, I've driven a Porsche. My friend's got one.
> It was incredible!
> It was amazing!
> I was a bit scared though.

8 | Media

1 **Talk about the news.**

How often do you watch, listen to or read about: local news, world news, business news?

Which newspapers, magazines, TV channels or websites do you read/watch for news?

Which English-language newspapers, news magazines and TV channels do you know?

2 **a** **Look at the screen from an international business and financial news channel, *City 24*. Match the descriptions (1–4) to the correct parts of the screen. Write a–d in the boxes.**

1 ☐ Here, you can read up-to-date business news.

2 ☐ This shows share prices and how much they have increased or decreased during the day. Green means a share price has gone up, red means it has gone down, and black means it hasn't changed.

3 ☐ These are the latest figures for the world's main stock market indexes: the Dow Jones, S&P 500, NASDAQ, FTSE, DAX, CAC 40, HSI and Nikkei.

4 ☐ This shows different information, for example exchange rates between major currencies such as the dollar, euro and yen. It can also show changes in stock market indexes during the last year, or, for example, shares that have risen or fallen the most during the day.

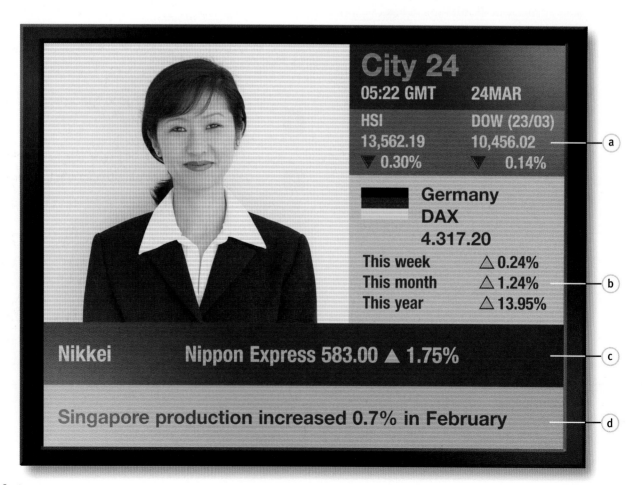

48

b Complete the sentences with words from 2a.

1 Investors buy and sell shares on the 'stock market' or 'stock _____'.

2 The Dow Jones is an American stock market _____ .

3 The dollar, euro and yen are all _____ .

4 The price of the euro to the dollar, for example, is an _____ _____ .

c Put these verbs from 2a into two groups.

> go down   go up   increase   decrease
> fall   rise

1 ▲ *go up* / _____ / _____

2 ▼ _____ / _____ / _____

d *Fall* and *rise* are both irregular verbs. What are (a) the past simple and (b) past participle forms?

1 fall: a *fell*   b _____

2 rise: a _____   b _____

e Vocabulary practice ⋯⟩ Page 101, Exercise 1.

f Look at the TV screen in 2a. Fill in the gaps with the correct form of verbs from 2c.

1 So far today, the HSI in Hong Kong has _____ by 0.30%.

2 Today, shares in the Japanese company Nippon Express have _____ by 1.75%.

3 This month, Germany's DAX index has _____ by 1.24%.

> *Present perfect:* **today, this week/ month/year**
>
> Share prices **have risen today.**
> The price **has gone up this week.**
> The index **has fallen this year.**
>
> ⋯⟩ **Grammar reference 4.2.5**

g Grammar practice ⋯⟩ Page 102, Exercise 2.

h Work with a partner. Describe things you've done:

- today
- this week
- this month
- this year

A I've made three phone calls today.

B I haven't made any.

3 a ▶▶ 49 Listen to an interview with Alan Styan, the chief executive of Geo-Core, on a business news programme. Answer the questions.

1 Has business been good for Geo-Core so far this year?

2 What does Geo-Core do?

3 Why is the oil price high?

b ▶▶ 49 Listen again and tick (✓) the correct boxes.

	▲ up	▼ down
1 Geo-Core's share price	☐	☐
2 The S&P 500 index	☐	☐
3 Geo-Core's profit	☐	☐
4 The oil price	☐	☐

c ▶▶ 49 Listen again and complete these sentences from the interview.

1 Your share price has _____ by _____ % in the first quarter of this year.

2 The S&P 500 has _____ by _____% so far this year.

3 Our profit has _____ by _____% this quarter.

d Look at the transcript for 3b on page 120 and check your answers.

4 Communication practice 22. Student A ⋯⟩ Page 84. Student B ⋯⟩ Page 92.

5 Work in groups. Talk about recent movements in share prices, oil prices and exchange rates.

> USEFUL LANGUAGE
>
> The share price has risen 32% this year.
> The company's sales have decreased.
> Oil prices have gone up this quarter.
> The company has done quite badly this year.
> Profits have increased again.
> Recently, the euro has fallen against the dollar.

1 a What are the advantages and disadvantages of buying and renting a home?

b Look at this chart. What information does it show?

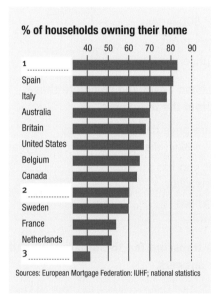

% of households owning their home

Sources: European Mortgage Federation: IUHF; national statistics

c Work with a partner. Can you fill in the missing countries on the chart?

> Japan   Germany
> Ireland

2 a Fill in the gaps in the article with the correct tense of the verbs.

UK property prices
REALITY TV AND ECONOMIC REALITY

Today, it seems half of the programmes on UK television [1] *are* *(be)* about houses. It all [2] _____ *(start)* in 2000, with the first reality TV show from the Big Brother house. But now it seems most programmes [3] _____ *(be)* about buying and selling homes. One reason for all the interest is the high price of property. House prices in the UK [4] _____ *(increase)* by about 75% in the last five years and by over 100% in the last ten.

Last year, a documentary series [5] _____ *(follow)* Britons who [6] _____ *(sell)* their houses and [7] _____ *(move)* to the continent. Most [8] _____ *(decide)* to move for better weather and less stress. But there was also the small question of money. In most parts of Europe property prices [9] _____ *(rise)* at the moment, but not as fast as in the UK. The price of a two-bedroom flat in London, for example, [10] _____ *(be)*

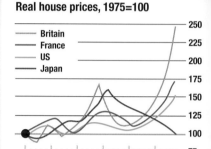

Real house prices, 1975=100

— Britain
— France
— US
— Japan

1975 80   85   90   95 2000 04

Sources: Japan Real Estate Institute; ODPM; OFHEO; government offices

currently equivalent to €600,000 — enough to buy a property ten times bigger in most parts of Europe.

TV and reality are usually very different, of course, and some economists think prices [11] _____ *(go)* down in the near future. If house prices [12] _____ *(fall)* suddenly, the UK economy [13] _____ *(be)* in serious trouble. But other economists think prices [14] _____ *(stay)* high, for a number of reasons.

b Now answer the questions about the article.

1 In the title, what word is a general name for houses and apartments?

2 In the UK, why have there been so many TV programmes about houses?

3 What's happening to prices in Europe, compared with the UK?

4 What are economists' forecasts for UK house prices?

c Grammar practice ···> Page 102, Exercise 3.

d Work with a partner. Ask and answer questions about property prices in your city or country. Think carefully about which tense to use.

1 are / property prices / high or low / at the moment ?

2 property prices / rise or fall / last year ?

3 property prices / rise / so far this year ?

3 a Match the pairs to complete the definitions. Write a–j in the boxes. Use a dictionary to help you, if necessary.

1 [g] The percentage of people without a job is the rate of

2 [ ] The amount prices increase in general, each year, is

3 [ ] If you get a loan from the bank, you

4 [ ] Banks give loans. They

5 [ ] The percentage a bank charges on a loan is the

6 [ ] Money you've borrowed is called

7 [ ] A loan to buy a house or an apartment is called a

8 [ ] When the economy grows very fast, it's called a

9 [ ] When the economy slows down for a time, it's a

10 [ ] When prices fall suddenly, it's called a

a lend (money).	**f** recession.
b borrow (money).	**g** unemployment.
c inflation.	**h** interest rate.
d mortgage.	**i** crash.
e debt.	**j** boom.

b ▶▶ 50 PRONUNCIATION Which three words in a–j have silent letters? Listen and check. Practise saying the words.

c ▶▶ 51 Listen to an interview with Roy Borg, an economist, talking about property prices and the economy. Does Roy agree (A) or disagree (D) with 1–4? Write A or D in the boxes.

1 Property prices are important in the economy. [ ]

2 Prices will continue to increase quickly. [ ]

3 Today, the situation is the same as in the late 1980s. [ ]

4 People will spend less in the future. [ ]

d Vocabulary practice ···> Page 102, Exercise 4.

e ▶▶ 51 Work with a partner. What reasons did Roy Borg give for his opinions in 3c? Listen again and check your answers.

4 Communication practice 23. Student A ···> Page 85. Student B ···> Page 92.

5 Work with a partner. Talk about the economy in your country.

What has the economic situation been like recently? What's it like now?

Do you think the economy will get better or worse in the next twelve months? Why?

USEFUL LANGUAGE

Unemployment is very high at the moment. It's over 12%.

Prices are increasing fast. Inflation is 5%.

Interest rates increased a lot last year. They went up 1.5%.

People have borrowed a lot of money, and will have to pay back large debts.

There's been a boom. Now, the question is, will there be a crash?

The economic situation isn't very good at the moment. We're in a recession.

1 **Talk about television.**

How often do you watch TV?

What did you watch last night?

Which channels do you watch most often?

Have you ever watched a TV programme in English?

2 a ▶▶ **52** **Naomi Blake, from the UK, is having lunch with her colleague Valerie Garde, in Paris. Listen to their conversation and answer the questions.**

1 Why do they start talking about TV programmes?

2 Which programme did Naomi watch last night?

3 Which two types of programme do they talk about?

b **In your country, do you have the types of programme Naomi and Valerie talked about? If so, what do you think of them?**

3 a **Is *Who Wants To Be A Millionaire?* on TV in your country? Do you watch it?**

b **Read about *Who Wants To Be A Millionaire?*. What does 'When's it on?' mean in the last line?**

c **Fill in the gaps.**

| channel presenter quiz programme show |

1 *Who Wants To Be A Millionaire?* is a TV ___quiz___ .

2 The show is on over a hundred television _____s.

3 The _____ has been extremely successful.

4 Each country has a different _____ .

d **Work with a partner. Take it in turns to describe *Who Wants To Be A Millionaire?*.**

e ▶▶ **53** **Listen to the second part of Naomi and Valerie's conversation. Answer the questions.**

1 What sort of channel is BBC Prime?

2 What programmes does Valerie find hard to understand?

3 Why does Naomi laugh?

4 What are two ways of showing films in another language?

Celador's global jackpot with *Who Wants To Be A Millionaire?*

Who wants to be a millionaire? Almost everyone – which is probably why the quiz show with the same name has become one of the world's most successful TV programmes. Celador, the British company that created the show, has sold it to channels in 104 countries.

The 'Millionaire' concept is the same worldwide; only the presenter, language and currency change. So far, 75 people have answered all 15 questions correctly to win the big prize. Japan has the most winners: 12 people have won ¥10 million. Why has the show been so successful? As one TV boss said, it's '… as simple and effective as a paper clip'. And 'money talks' in every language.

| 50:50 | | |

15	£1 MILLION
14	£500,000
13	£250,000
12	£125,000
11	£64,000
10	£32,000
9	£16,000
8 ◆	£8,000
7 ◆	£4,000
6 ◆	£2,000
5 ◆	£1,000
4 ◆	£500
3 ◆	£300
2 ◆	£200
1 ◆	£100

f ▶▶ **53** **Listen again. Complete the sentences about programmes on BBC Prime.**

1 *The Weakest Link* is a .... show.
2 Michael Parkinson presents a .... show.
3 *Teletubbies* is a ....'s programme.
4 *EastEnders* is a ....

g **Look at the transcript for 3e on page 121 and check your answers.**

4 **a** **Fill in the gaps 1–10 in the TV schedule for 'Tonight on 1'.**

> comedy   documentary   film   news
> soap opera   talk show   weather   dubbed
> starring   presented

b **Which programmes from the schedule would/wouldn't you like to watch? Ask other people in the group.**

c **Vocabulary practice ···> Page 102, Exercise 5.**

d **Work in pairs. Take it in turns to think of a TV show and describe it. Can your partner guess what it is?**

A It's a comedy. It's on Wednesday evenings.
B Who stars in it?
A Sam Rockwell
B Is it ...?

5 **Communication practice 24. ···> Page 85. Work with a partner.**

6 **Talk about television programmes.**
What sort of TV programmes are popular in your country?
What types of programme do you like most? Why?
In your opinion, what are the worst programmes on TV? Why don't you like them?
Do you think watching TV is good or bad for children? Why?

USEFUL LANGUAGE

Did you watch that quiz show last night?
Do you have ... in your country? It's a reality TV show.
Have you ever seen that programme about buying property abroad?
I watched an interesting documentary about China last night.
What channel is it on?
Have you got satellite or cable TV?
Do you get the ... channel?
Does the film have subtitles or is it dubbed?

Tonight on 1

7.00 **World** [1] *news* ....
7.25 [2] .... **forecast**
7.30 **Oasis** [3] .... about developers in the Gulf States who turn desert into luxury property developments.
8.00 **Chandler Street** [4] .... Nancy tells Jim her secret. Gary's pet rats escape into the street ...
8.30 **The Big Quiz** More contestants go for the big prize. [5] .... by Shane Black.
9.00 **Funny Man** [6] .... with laugh-a-minute Jerry Man.
9.30 **White Nights** [7] .... with Julian White. Guest: singer Nelly Dean.
10.30 **The Final Push** [8] .... , 2005. Spanish thriller [9] .... Jordi Pons. [10] ....

7.15
7.35
7.45 .... from the
8.15 S.............
      C.............
8.45 Go.............
      yes.............
9.30 The.............
      pres.............   ic show
9.55 Zone.............   a
11.15 Chan.............
      the fig.............
      Samue.............
11.30 Late Ne.............   alk
12.00 Midnigh.............
      through ....

7.00 **Blue Light**
7.30 **Shadowla**
8.00 **Local Lin**
8.45 **Webmas** knowled
9.15 **Who's W** A day in
9.55 **A Sport** Special
10.05 **Knight**
11.35 **Grand** F1 high
12.45 **Dark C**
1.00 **Flight** futuris

9 | Strategy

9.1 | Describing a business concept

GRAMMAR — Passive: present simple, past simple

VOCABULARY — Marketing and advertising

1 a Talk to a partner about advertising.

What are your favourite adverts?

In your opinion, what makes a good advert?

b Match the words to the photos of different types of advertising. Write a–e in the boxes.

1 [d] press ads
2 [ ] billboard ads
3 [ ] TV commercials
4 [ ] sponsorship
5 [ ] product placement

2 a ▶▶ 54 Listen to Amy Venn, the new marketing manager of Sway, a clothing company. She's making a presentation to the directors. Which types of advertising is Sway using at the moment?

b ▶▶ 54 Listen again and answer the questions.

1 Which age group are Sway targeting with their press advertising?
2 Which sports does Amy mention when she talks about sponsorship?
3 Why does Sway spend so much on advertising?
4 How does Amy suggest cutting costs?

c Look at the transcript for 2b on page 122 and check your answers.

d Write the verbs from these nouns.

Noun	Verb
1 advertising	....
2 marketing	....
3 promotion	....
4 sponsorship	....

e ▶▶ 55 PRONUNCIATION Listen and repeat 1–4. For each word, underline the stressed syllable.

f Vocabulary practice ···▶ Page 102, Exercise 1.

g Work with a partner. Discuss the advantages and disadvantages of the different types of advertising.

3 a ▶▶ 56 Amy Venn is talking to a junior colleague about product placement. Listen and answer the questions.

1 Do product placements always show the company logo?
2 What product placements are very expensive?
3 What did the first product placements advertise?
4 Which company had a product placement in the film *Forrest Gump*?

b ▶▶ **56** **These sentences from the conversation use the passive. Listen again and fill in the gaps.**

1 The products ___*are*___ ___*seen*___ in films and TV programmes.
2 Often, products _____ _____ to the film company for free.
3 Sometimes, the film company _____ _____ by the advertiser.
4 Sometimes, the name of a product _____ _____ by an actor.
5 I think the first placements _____ _____ in films in the 1960s, for cigarettes.
6 Did you see *Forrest Gump*? The Apple placement _____ _____ very well in that.

c **Look at the transcript for 3b on page 122 and check your answers.**

Passive: present simple, past simple

Active	Apple **uses** product placement.
Passive	Product placement **is used** by Apple.
Active	Companies **show** products in films.
Passive	Products **are shown** in films.
Active	Millions of viewers **saw** the film.
Passive	The film **was seen** by millions of viewers.

···❯ **Grammar reference 7**

---

d **Now fill in the gaps in the article about Apple. Use the passive.**

e **Are these sentences true (T) or false (F)?**

1 A computer with an Apple logo was shown in *Forrest Gump*. ☐
2 *Forrest Gump* was watched by tens of millions of people. ☐
3 Films are often helped by the image of the Apple brand. ☐
4 Apple was given an award for increasing its market share. ☐

f **Can you think of any other examples of product placement? Discuss them with a partner.**

g **Grammar practice** ···❯ **Page 102, Exercise 2.**

4 Communication practice 25. Student A ···❯ Page 85. Student B ···❯ Page 92.

5 **Talk about product placement.**

Do you think product placement can be more effective than advertising? Say why.

In your opinion, what's the difference between good and bad product placement?

USEFUL LANGUAGE

In return for a payment, the product is shown in the film.

In big films, the logos on products are seen by millions of viewers.

Product placement was used for the first time in the 1960s.

Has Apple enjoyed the fruits of product placement?

In the movie *Forrest Gump*, Forrest (Tom Hanks) receives a letter telling him that he's become a millionaire from his shares in Apple. Forrest is surprised to learn, not just that he's rich, but that 'a fruit company' has done so well. The Apple logo on Forrest's letter [1] ___*was seen*___ *(see)* by over 75 million people in 1994. Since then, the computer firm has become a star of the big and small screen. Nowadays, its products [2] _____ *(show)* regularly in films and big American TV series.

Apple has become part of the Hollywood scenery for a good reason – it has the right image. When a new Apple laptop [3] _____ *(use)* by a star, it doesn't just help with promotion of the brand – it also makes the film or programme look fashionable.

In 2004, Apple [4] _____ *(give)* a 'Lifetime Achievement Award for Product Placement' by Interbrand's brandchannel.com website. But that doesn't mean the company's product placements have resulted in huge sales. Abram Sauer from brandchannel.com thinks Apple's market share (about 2% of the world computer market) is low for a company whose products [5] _____ *(promote)* so much on screen. He says this 'raises huge questions' about product placement, and that '... at worst, product placement doesn't really work at all.'

1 a What do you know about the 'dot.com boom' of the late 1990s?

b Read the review. Why do you think the book is called *boo hoo*?

c Read the review again and answer the questions.

1 What is the book about?

2 What sort of company was boo?

3 Who is Ernst Malmsten?

BUSINESS BOOK REVIEW

boo hoo: $135 million, 18 months ... a dot.com story from concept to catastrophe
Ernst Malmsten, Erik Portanger and Charles Drazin

If you want a change from books about business success, *boo hoo* is perfect. It tells the incredible-but-true story of boo.com, an Internet sports clothing retailer. The firm was set up in 1998 by Swedish entrepreneurs Ernst Malmsten and Kajsa Leander. Both were 28 years old, and had a strong track record in business (in the mid-90s, they built a successful Internet book-selling firm in Sweden). But their ambitions for boo were much bigger ...

d Work in pairs. Can you complete the chart of boo's history? Fill in the gaps 1–5 with the missing text a–e.

a Boo.com was finally launched on November 3rd. The company started making money ...

b The founders travelled all over the world, meeting new investors. They needed finance for computer equipment, and to recruit workers. They worked extremely hard, but lived well – they stayed in the best hotels, sometimes flew on Concorde and even rented a private jet.

c Sales didn't reach forecasts and costs were still too high. On May 18th, boo closed its website. A short time later, the firm went bankrupt.

d Before they set up boo, the founders planned their strategy carefully.

e Boo expanded fast. It opened offices in New York, Munich, Paris and Stockholm. The firm hired 200 employees. By the summer, salary costs were $1.4 million per month. But the website launch was delayed, due to technical problems.

1998 → ¹ *d*
- They needed to find investors to raise finance for the company.
- They intended to launch boo.com in May 1999.
- By the end of 1999, they aimed to have offices in eight countries.
- In early 2000, they hoped to list boo on the stock market.
→ Boo was set up at the end of the year. The company opened its first office in London.

1999 → ² ....
→ The firm invested in expensive equipment. It spent $2 million on a server, for example.
→ ³ ....
→ Newspapers and magazines around the world printed stories about the founders. The boo brand quickly became well known. But the website still wasn't open ...
→ ⁴ ....

2000 → ... but not fast enough. Boo had to cut costs. In January, it laid off 130 workers.
→ ⁵ ....

e Match the definitions to the words a–i.

1 start a new business   a invest
2 find money for a business   b lay off
3 put money into a business   c set up
4 put (a product) on the market   d go bankrupt
5 grow (a business)   e cut costs
6 employ (workers)   f raise finance
7 spend less   g expand
8 fire/dismiss (workers)   h hire
9 close the business because of debt   i launch

f Vocabulary practice ···> Page 103, Exercise 3.

g What do you think boo's biggest mistake was? Discuss with a partner.

2 **a** ▶▶ 57 Listen to Tony Ellston, an entrepreneur, talking to Jane Rye, an investment banker. She's advising him on business strategy. Are these sentences true (T) or false (F)?

1 Tony's business has had problems recently.   *F*
2 He's planning to build a new factory.   ☐
3 He needs to hire some employees.   ☐
4 He wants to borrow money from the bank.   ☐
5 Jane asks Tony about his long-term future.   ☐

b Fill in the gaps in these sentences from the conversation.

> carefully easily gradually hard quickly
> significantly well

1 The business has done _____well_____ over the last three years.
2 To expand _____ , I need more than just money.
3 I'm sure you know what it's like to work _____ , seven days a week.
4 ... each year, your job changes _____ .
5 ... obviously, that's a big change, so your job needs to change _____ .
6 It's not a decision you can make _____ .
7 You need to think about your future _____ .

c ▶▶ 57 Listen again and check your answers.

> *Adverbs of manner*
>
> It's not a **quick** job. We can't do it **quickly**.
> Our growth has been **gradual**. We've grown **gradually**.
> He's a **hard** worker. He works **hard**. (*irregular*)
>
> ···> **Grammar reference 10**

d Grammar practice ···> Page 103, Exercise 4.

e ▶▶ 58 PRONUNCIATION Listen and repeat. Is the stress in the adjectives and adverbs the same or different?

1 careful > carefully
2 easy > easily
3 gradual > gradually
4 significant > significantly

f Work with a partner. Make sentences about yourself using each of these adverbs.

● carefully ● hard ● well
● quickly ● easily

I always check figures carefully.

3 Communication practice 26 ···> Page 85. Work with a partner.

> USEFUL LANGUAGE
>
> We need to plan our strategy carefully.
>
> We've grown quickly since we set up the company.
>
> We're expanding gradually. We're hiring new workers.
>
> We want to invest in new equipment. We need to raise finance.
>
> Last year they had to cut costs significantly. They laid off 40 workers.

1 **a** **Talk about the Internet.**

How often do you use the Internet?

What do you use the Internet for?

What websites do you visit most often?

How has the Internet made life easier in the last ten years?

b ▶▶ **59** **Listen to three people talking about what they do on the Internet. Answer the questions.**

Person 1 **1** What does he like about the Internet?

2 What's the problem with using the Internet?

Person 2 **3** How does the Internet help save her time?

4 What does she think about security online?

Person 3 **5** What sort of website does he talk about?

6 What can you do at the website?

c **Match the pairs to make sentences.**

1 ☐ *e* To enter some sites, you have to type a secret word called a

2 ☐ At some sites, you can complete a form with your details to

3 ☐ These days, most software is easy to

4 ☐ Before you enter a password, you usually type your

5 ☐ When you're registered at a site, you enter your password to

6 ☐ To look for information on the web you can use a

7 ☐ Sites that accept payments by credit card use a

8 ☐ When you get large files from the Internet, they take time to

9 ☐ To use a search engine, you type in a

10 ☐ If you pay to have access to a website, we say you

a download.	**f** register.
b install.	**g** search engine.
c keyword.	**h** secure server.
d log in.	**i** join/become a member.
e password.	**j** user name.

d **Vocabulary practice ···>** Page 103, Exercise 5.

e ▶▶ **60** **PRONUNCIATION** Listen and repeat the words ending in *-er*. How do we pronounce the *-er* sound?

regist<u>er</u>   serv<u>er</u>   memb<u>er</u>   us<u>er</u>

f **Work with a partner. Discuss the questions.**

Do you ever download software from the Internet?

How do you search for information on the web?

Are you registered at, or are you a member of, any websites?

Do you sometimes use secure servers?

2 **a** **Look at three extracts (a–c), from the website of a magazine. Work with a partner to fill in the gaps, using the words a–j from 1c.**

a

For free access to selected articles from the current print edition of the magazine, you need to [1] _register_ .
Full access to current and past articles is only available to members.

<u>Click here</u> to complete the registration form.

If you're a registered user, please log in below.

User name [＿＿＿＿＿＿＿＿＿] [2]＿＿＿＿ [＿＿＿＿＿＿＿＿＿] ▶

[3]＿＿＿＿ now for full access. Membership costs only £10 a month and the first month is FREE.
Click here to pay by credit card using our [4]＿＿＿＿ ＿＿＿＿ .

b

Use the [5]＿＿＿＿ ＿＿＿＿ to search for current and past articles.

Enter one or more [6]＿＿＿＿s. [＿＿＿＿＿＿＿] ▶

<u>FAQ</u> If you can't find what you're looking for, or need help, go to our frequently asked questions page.

c

To read this page from the print edition, you need Adobe Reader. <u>Click here</u> to [7]＿＿＿＿ Adobe Reader free.

---

b Read the web pages again and answer the questions.

1 What's the difference between registering and becoming a member?
2 How do you register at the site?
3 Do you have to pay to register?
4 How much does it cost to become a member?
5 What can you use the search engine for?
6 What does FAQ stand for?

c Complete the online registration form.

Please take a few minutes to register.

Enter your email address: [1] [t.yelland@tby.o-net.com]
(We will send you an email to confirm your address.)

Choose a password: [2] [＿＿＿＿＿＿＿]
(4–20 characters, case-sensitive, no spaces)

Confirm password: [3] [＿＿＿＿＿＿＿]

What country do you live in? [4] [＿＿＿＿＿＿＿＿＿]

Post code (optional): [5] [＿＿＿＿＿]

☐ Tick this box if you would like to receive regular email updates from us.

☐ Tick this box if you would like to receive messages from other companies approved by us.

Please read our <u>privacy policy</u>.

d Imagine your password is 'Elephant'. Why can't you enter the website if you type 'elephant'?

3 Communication practice 27 ···⟩ Page 86. Work with a partner.

USEFUL LANGUAGE

To register at this site, please enter your details on the form below.

To log in, enter your user name and password.

This section is only available to members.

Use the search engine to search for information using keywords.

If you have a question, see our frequently asked questions page.

Click here to download and install the software.

10 | Solutions

10.1 | Discussing ideas

GRAMMAR Second conditional

VOCABULARY Suggestions

Das Modell Leonardo 150?

---

1 **Talk about creativity.**

How creative are you?

How important is creativity for your work?

Do you use your creative skills enough?

2 **a** ▶▶ **61** **Listen to a team meeting at Optiplain, a manufacturer of blank CDs and CD packaging. What are the team discussing? What suggestions do they make?**

b ▶▶ **61** **Listen again. Fill in the gaps in these extracts from the meeting.**

1 **A** ... some new ideas. How __could__ we make the product better?

2 **A** Any suggestions?

B _____ about changing the packaging? We could change the material.

3 **A** Yeah. Packaging material. OK.

C _____ about changing the size?

4 **C** No, the pack. Why _____ we sell more CDs in a pack, for example?

5 **A** So, bigger packs. They could be smaller, as well.

B Why _____ sell big boxes – big storage boxes ...?

6 **B** Then you wouldn't need packaging.

A So that _____ be a new product. A storage box.

7 **A** That's a good idea. We _____ use that idea with the storage box.

8 **A** That's an _____ idea.

c **Look at the transcript for 2b on page 123 and check your answers.**

d **Vocabulary practice ···> Page 103, Exercise 1.**

e **Work with a partner. Imagine you're in the meeting at Optiplain. Use different expressions from 2b to make these suggestions.**

We could ... . Why don't we ...? How about ..? Why not ...?

- produce CDs in different colours
- use tubes for packaging
- make square CDs
- look for new places to sell CDs
- think about new ways to advertise

3 **a** **Have you ever heard of Edward de Bono? Read the text. Can you complete the title of his book?**

Serious Creativity: Using the Power of L_____ Thinking to Create N_____ I_____

Edward de Bono

It is often said that, to think of new ideas, you need to 'think laterally'. Most people know this means 'think differently', but don't know it's a specific technique developed by Edward de Bono. Dr de Bono, who first used lateral thinking in 1967, is a leading expert in thinking skills. He has worked as a consultant for companies and governments all over the world. He has also written 46 books, including *Serious Creativity*, which explains how to use lateral thinking to create ideas.

What would happen if ...?

One of Edward de Bono's creative thinking techniques is 'provocation'. In simple terms, this means making crazy or impossible suggestions to help you think laterally.

b What skills and techniques has Edward de Bono developed?

c ▶▶ **62** Two colleagues from the research and development department at Optiplain are using lateral thinking to create new ideas. Listen and fill in the gaps 1–4.

could	would	couldn't	wouldn't

↓ – Let's think about packaging and storing CDs.

a ☐ – OK. What would happen if you made packaging from water?

↓ – You ¹_____ only use water if you froze CDs in ice.

↓ – Obviously, you ²_____ use ice for packaging CDs to sell in shops.

b ☐
↓ – No. But let's think about the possible advantages of putting CDs in ice.

c ☐ – If you stored them in ice, it ³_____ protect them from fire or thieves.

↓ – You could store important data safely on CD-ROMs in big blocks of ice.

↓ – You could build an 'ice data bank' for storing data safely and permanently.

↓ – And if it was in a cold country it ⁴_____ be expensive.

d Now fill in boxes a, b and c with these terms:

specific ideas	provocation	lateral thinking

e Talk about the discussion at Optiplain.

What idea is created?

What does it show about lateral thinking?

> **Second conditional**
>
> **If** we **did** that, we**'d** have problems. (**we'd = we would**)
>
> **If** we **used** plastic, we **could** make it lighter.
>
> ⋯▸ **Grammar reference 6.2**

f ▶▶ **63** PRONUNCIATION Listen and repeat the sentences in the grammar box. Copy the stress and intonation.

g Grammar practice ⋯▸ Page 103, Exercise 2.

h Work with a partner. Discuss what you'd do, or what would happen, in these situations.

1 If my ideas were always better than my colleagues' …

2 If a colleague stole one of my ideas …

3 If a boss often told employees their ideas were stupid …

4 If I invented a water engine, for cars, …

4 Communication practice 28 ⋯▸ Page 86. Work with a partner.

5 Talk about lateral thinking.

Do you think lateral thinking works?

Do you think you could use lateral thinking in your job?

> USEFUL LANGUAGE
>
> We could change the packaging.
> Why don't we use a different material?
> Why not have paper packaging?
> What about having a number on each CD?
> How about selling big boxes of CDs?
> Good idea. That's an interesting idea.
> If we did that, it would cost less.

1 **a** Read the comments about decision making. Which do you agree and disagree with? Say why.

1 'I think it's best to tell people what you really think of their suggestions, and to be direct.'

2 'If you don't agree with someone's idea, it's important not to criticise their suggestion.'

3 'In companies, it's best to make group decisions. It's important that all the team agrees.'

4 'In the end, one person has to make a decision, even if the others in the team don't agree.'

b ▶▶ **64** Sandra Franks has worked as a training manager in several international companies. Listen to an interview with her. What general advice does she give about:

• politeness? • criticism?
• changing how you communicate?

c ▶▶ **64** Listen again. Underline the correct words so that the sentences are true.

1 In Germany, you *should/ shouldn't* be very direct.

2 In the UK, you *have to/ don't have to* agree all the time.

3 In Japan, you *should/shouldn't* criticise people directly.

4 In Japanese companies, they often *have to/don't have to* make decisions in groups.

d Work with a partner. Do you agree with Sandra? Compare her views with any experiences you have.

should, have to

I think we **should** develop this product.
In my opinion, we **shouldn't** make a decision yet.
We **have to** make a decision soon.
We **don't have to** decide now.

···> Grammar reference 9.1 and 9.2

e Grammar practice ···> Page 103, Exercise 3.

f ▶▶ **65** PRONUNCIATION Listen and repeat. What happens when *should* is followed by a vowel?

1 We should_act now.

2 You should_ask Mike about that.

3 We should_invest in a new factory.

g Work with a partner. Discuss things you should/shouldn't do in these situations.

1 If you visit a customer …

2 If a customer visits you …

3 When you go to a job interview …

4 When you give a presentation …

2 **a** Read the article. What technique is described and why was it developed?

Edward de Bono's Six Thinking Hats...

In the West, suggestions are usually criticised immediately. Criticism is seen as the best way to improve ideas and make good decisions. In Edward de Bono's view, this is wrong. He believes criticism is important, but shouldn't take priority. To solve this problem, he developed the 'Six Thinking Hats', which companies such as IBM and DuPont have used successfully. When the technique is used in a meeting, the chairperson asks the group to 'put on' imaginary hats of different colours. Each hat is 'worn' for a specific type of thinking. Only one is for criticism.

b Match the pairs to describe the 'Six Thinking Hats'.

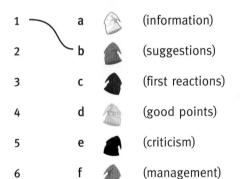

1 Look at information.

2 Make new suggestions.

3 Give immediate reactions to ideas.

4 Say what's good about ideas.

5 Criticise ideas.

6 Manage the discussion.

a Create ideas.

b Conclude and move on.

c Discuss only the advantages.

d Discuss only the disadvantages.

e Discuss only the facts.

f Discuss first feelings about the ideas.

c ▶▶ **66** The directors of Altora, a drinks company, are considering opening a new factory. Listen to six extracts from the meeting. Match each extract (1–6) to one of the 'Six Thinking Hats'.

1 a (information)

2 b (suggestions)

3 c (first reactions)

4 d (good points)

5 e (criticism)

6 f (management)

d Fill in the gaps in these sentences from the meeting.

> benefits idea option proposals recommend worried

1 I think we should consider that _option_ . It's a possibility.

2 There would be a lot of _____ if we just had one plant.

3 I think we should just consider two or three _____ .

4 I don't think it would be a good _____ to spend so much.

5 I'm _____ about the economic situation. I think it's too uncertain.

6 I just wouldn't _____ such a big investment.

e ▶▶ **67** Listen and check your answers.

f Vocabulary practice ⸱⸱⸱> Page 104, Exercise 4.

3 Communication practice 29 ⸱⸱⸱> Page 86. Work in groups of three or four.

4 Talk about the 'Six Thinking Hats'.

Do you think the technique works?

In your opinion, which hats are the easiest and most difficult to 'wear'?

Do you think the technique would work in your company?

> USEFUL LANGUAGE
>
> Let's discuss this proposal.
> This idea would give us several benefits.
> I think we should consider other options.
> We have to make sure it's not too expensive.
> I'm worried about the cost.
> I wouldn't recommend doing that. I'd recommend the other option.
> I don't think it's a good idea to do that.

1 Talk about transport in your country.

What's the most reliable way to travel?

What's the cheapest way to travel?

Are there many problems with the trains/buses /roads?

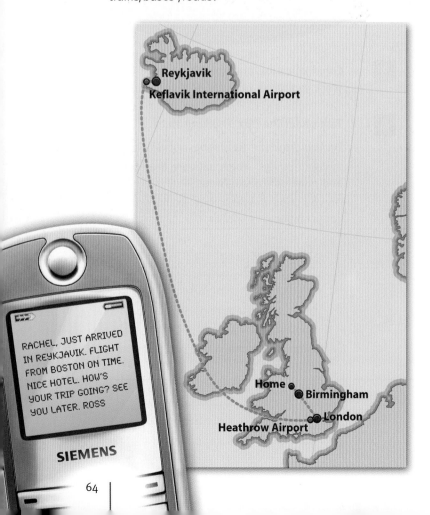

Reykjavik
Keflavik International Airport

Home
Birmingham
Heathrow Airport
London

RACHEL, JUST ARRIVED IN REYKJAVIK. FLIGHT FROM BOSTON ON TIME. NICE HOTEL. HOW'S YOUR TRIP GOING? SEE YOU LATER. ROSS

SIEMENS

2 **a** Rachel Barden is travelling to a conference in Iceland. Read the text messages she sent to her colleague, Ross Owen, during the trip. Put the messages in the correct order. Number them 1–5.

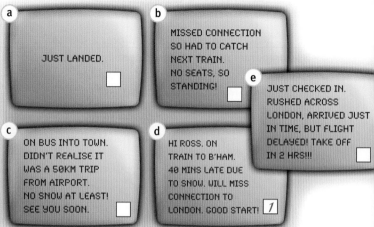

a JUST LANDED. ☐

b MISSED CONNECTION SO HAD TO CATCH NEXT TRAIN. NO SEATS, SO STANDING! ☐

e JUST CHECKED IN. RUSHED ACROSS LONDON, ARRIVED JUST IN TIME, BUT FLIGHT DELAYED! TAKE OFF IN 2 HRS!!! ☐

c ON BUS INTO TOWN. DIDN'T REALISE IT WAS A 50KM TRIP FROM AIRPORT. NO SNOW AT LEAST! SEE YOU SOON. ☐

d HI ROSS. ON TRAIN TO B'HAM. 40 MINS LATE DUE TO SNOW. WILL MISS CONNECTION TO LONDON. GOOD START! ☐ *1*

b Answer the questions about Rachel's trip.

1 Where did Rachel change trains?

2 Why did she arrive late in London?

3 On which part of her trip did she have to stand?

4 How did she get from the airport to Reykjavik?

5 Why is she surprised when she arrives in Iceland?

c Find words in the text messages to complete 1–8.

1 change from one train to another = a *connection*

2 take a train = ... a train

3 arrive too late for a train = ... a train

4 late = ...

5 what planes do when they leave = ...

6 what planes do when they arrive = ...

7 what you do before a flight = ...

8 what you do when you're in a hurry = ...

d Work with a partner. Sum up Rachel's trip. Say what happened, and what problems she had, during each part of the journey.

3 a ▶▶ **68** Listen to Rachel having a conversation during her trip. What city and place is she in?

b ▶▶ **68** Listen again. Are these sentences true (T) or false (F)?

1 The next train is at 9.30. [F]
2 Rachel's ticket is OK for the next train. [ ]
3 She could book a seat on the next train. [ ]
4 She could go first class if she paid more. [ ]
5 She changes her ticket. [ ]
6 The next train is running on time. [ ]

c Fill in the gaps.

> cancel refund supplement upgrade valid

1 A Do I get my money back?
  B Yes, we can give you a _refund_ .
2 I can't go, so I want to _____ the reservation.
3 Can I _____ the ticket from second class to first class?
4 A Would it cost any more?
  B Yes. You'd have to pay a _____ .
5 You can't use that ticket on this train. It's not _____ .

d Vocabulary practice ⋯▸ Page 104, Exercise 5.

e ▶▶ **69** PRONUNCIATION Listen and repeat. How do we say the underlined sounds? Tick (✓) the boxes.

	/ʃ/	/tʃ/
1 cancellation	✓	
2 catch		
3 connection		
4 check in		
5 change		
6 reservation		

4 ▶▶ **70** Listen to three conversations about travel problems. Make notes in the chart to sum up the problem and describe the solution.

1	Location	*on a train*
	Problem	
	Solution	
2	Location	
	Problem	
	Solution	
3	Location	
	Problem	
	Solution	

5 Communication practice 30. Student A ⋯▸ page 86. Student B ⋯▸ page 93.

6 Talk about travel problems you've had, for example:
- long delays and cancelled departures
- missing important trains or flights
- problems with tickets and reservations
- traffic jams

USEFUL LANGUAGE

I've missed my connection. Can I catch the next train?
Is this ticket valid on the next train?
If I cancel the ticket, will I get a refund?
If I change the reservation, will I have to pay a supplement?
Are there any seats in first class? Can I upgrade?
Is the train running on time?
The flight's delayed.

11.1	Describing how things work	GRAMMAR	Prepositions: position and movement
		VOCABULARY	Size and dimensions

1 **a** **Work with a partner. Look at the title of the article and photos. What can you say about Maglevs?**

b **Read the article and answer the questions.**

1 Which two places are connected by the Maglev line?

2 What's the main difference between Maglevs and normal trains?

3 What's the best thing about Maglev technology?

4 What's Maglev's main disadvantage?

c **<u>Underline</u> the correct words so that the sentences are true.**

1 To get to the airport, you need to go *into/<u>out of</u>* the centre of Shanghai.

2 To get to the airport, you get *on/off* the Maglev at Longyang Road Station.

3 The track takes a direct route. It goes *across/around* the city.

4 The track is at a high level. It goes *under/over* the streets of Shanghai.

5 The Maglev travels just *below/above* the track.

6 The Maglev is lifted *up/down* by magnetic force.

7 The Maglev is pushed *along/through* the track by magnets.

430 KM/H 'MAGLEV' AIRPORT SHUTTLE TAKES OFF IN SHANGHAI

When you get on the train at Longyang Road Station in Shanghai, you know it won't be long before take-off – and not just because you're going direct to Pudong International Airport. Thanks to the city's new 'Maglev' train, you don't have to wait to get on a plane before you leave the ground – you take off before you come out of the station.

Maglev is short for 'magnetic levitation'. The system was developed by the German firm Transrapid. The train is lifted off the track, to a height of about 1 cm, by electromagnets. It's then pushed along the line by the same magnetic force, up to its maximum speed. The advantage of 'flying' above the track is that there's no need for wheels or other moving parts, which use a lot of energy. This means the train can travel extremely fast: up to 430 km/h. If Maglev technology is economical to run, however, it's not cheap to build. The cost of the 30 km track across Shanghai was a huge $1.2 billion.

Will Maglev change the future of train travel? Clearly, costs need to come down before long-distance tracks are built. But many believe the technology will take off because of its high-speed potential. Travelling the full length of Germany or France, for example, would take just over two hours on a Maglev.

Prepositions: position and movement

The Maglev travels **above** the track.
The train is lifted **up** by magnetic force.
You get **off** the train at the airport.

···> **Grammar reference 11.1 and 11.2**

d **Grammar practice** ···> Page 104, Exercise 1.

e Work with a partner. Say as much as you can about what these things do and how they work. Use prepositions from 1c.

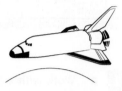

helicopters   submarines   hovercrafts   car ferries   spaceships

2

a Look at the drawing of a component from a high-speed train. With a partner, fill in the gaps with the dimensions.

1 Length of plate: It's _1.2 m_ long.
2 Width of plate: It's .... wide.
3 Thickness of plate: It's .... thick.
4 Height of tube: It's .... high.
5 Diameter of tube: It's .... wide.
6 Total weight: It weighs ....

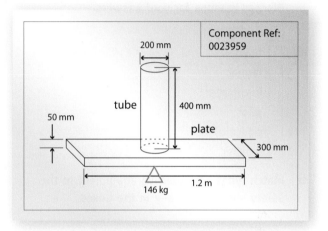

Component Ref: 0023959
200 mm
tube
400 mm
50 mm
plate
300 mm
146 kg
1.2 m

b **►► 71** Lindsey Gamble, an engineer, is giving a presentation at a conference on rail transport technology. She's talking about high-speed train design. Listen and answer the questions.

1 What's the first dimension train designers have to look at?
2 What's the problem with standard rail tracks?
3 Why aren't trains very economical?

c Can you complete these sentences from the conversation? Underline the correct words.

1 How *long/wide* is the track? What's the distance between the rails?
2 The *height/weight* of the train is also limited by the width of the track.
3 So, for better stability, a *wide/narrow* track is better.
4 To help the train stay on the track, you make it quite *heavy/light* …
5 Just look at the big, *thick/thin* pieces of steel used in trains …

d **►► 72** Listen and check your answers.

e Vocabulary practice ···> Page 104, Exercise 2.

f **►► 73** PRONUNCIATION Listen and repeat the words. Are the underlined sounds the same or different?

		the same	different
1	w<u>i</u>de	w<u>i</u>dth	☐	✓
2	narr<u>ow</u>	shall<u>ow</u>	☐	☐
3	h<u>ei</u>ght	w<u>ei</u>ght	☐	☐
4	ar<u>ou</u>nd	thr<u>ou</u>gh	☐	☐
5	le<u>ng</u>th	de<u>p</u>th	☐	☐
6	thick<u>ness</u>	<u>less</u>	☐	☐

3 Communication practice 31. Student A ···> Page 87. Student B ···> Page 93.

4 Take it in turns to describe an object in the room for your partner to guess.

A It's about thirty centimetres wide. It's two and a half metres above the floor.
B Is it the clock?

USEFUL LANGUAGE

What's the length/width/height/thickness?
How long/wide/high/thick is it?
Is the track short/narrow/low//thin?
What's the weight of the train? Is it light/heavy?

1 **a** Work with a partner. Put the jobs in order of how dangerous you think they are. Write 1–7 in the boxes (1 = the most dangerous). Discuss reasons for your answers.

- [ ] accountant
- [ ] builder
- [ ] farmer
- [ ] fire fighter
- [ ] pilot
- [ ] police officer
- [ ] teacher

b Match types of protective equipment to the safety signs. Write a–g in the boxes.

1 [f] mask
2 [ ] hard hat
3 [ ] ear protection
4 [ ] eye protection
5 [ ] protective gloves
6 [ ] high visibility clothing
7 [ ] protective shoes or boots

c With a partner, give examples of jobs where workers need to wear the protective equipment in 1b. Say why they need it.

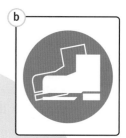

2 **a** Work with a partner. Talk about safety for airport employees who work on the tarmac around planes. Make lists of the dangers. What safety precautions do workers need to take?

Dangers	Safety precautions

b ▶▶ 74 Listen to Dennis Addie, a safety officer, giving a training course to some trainee airport workers. Compare what he says to your lists in 2a.

c ▶▶ **74** **Listen again and answer the questions.**

1 What's the biggest danger on the tarmac?

2 Why is the danger in question 1 worse at airports?

3 Which workers need to wear ear protection?

4 What's the problem with ear protection?

5 What other words does Dennis use for *danger* and *dangerous*?

d **Look at the transcript for 2b on page 124. Find words to complete 1–6.**

1 stop accidents from happening = _prevent_ / _____ accidents

2 take action to stop accidents = take _____

3 you can do it if you want = you're _____ to do it.

4 it's not permitted = you're _____ _____ to do it.

5 safety rules = _____ and safety _____

6 standard ways of working = standard _____

e Vocabulary practice ···> Page 104, Exercise 3.

3 **a** **Work with a partner. Read these sentences. Use a dictionary to help you if necessary. Do you think they are true (T) or false (F)?**

1 Airline pilots have to be over 28 years old. ☐

2 For international flights, the pilots have to be able to speak English. ☐

3 The pilot has to walk around the plane and check it before each flight. ☐

4 A plane can't take off if there are small cracks in the wings. ☐

5 Planes are never allowed to take off if an engine isn't working. ☐

b ▶▶ **75** **Now listen to an interview with Mike Collins, an airline pilot. Check your answers to 3a.**

c ▶▶ **75** **Listen again. Fill in the gaps with *must* or *mustn't*.**

1 It's all about procedures, in fact. Pilots _must_ know exactly what to do in all situations.

2 ... you need a minimum number of hours flying time. You _____ have at least 1,500 hours.

3 We have a lot of checklists. There are things you _____ always check before each flight. You _____ take off until you've checked everything.

4 If you're above a certain speed, the procedure is, you _____ try to stop.

---

must

All pilots **must** have a licence.
(= They have to have one.)

You **mustn't** carry dangerous items on planes. (= You're not allowed to.)

···> **Grammar reference 9.3**

---

d Grammar practice ···> Page 104, Exercise 4.

e **With a partner, make a list of things you must/mustn't do when you go to an airport or get on a plane. Compare your suggestions with another pair of students.**

You must check in two hours before your flight leaves. You mustn't ... .

4 Communication practice 32 ···> Page 87. Work with a partner.

5 **Talk about safety in your job, company or industry, or another industry you know about.**

What are the main dangers?

What safety precautions must workers take and what procedures must they follow?

USEFUL LANGUAGE

What are the health and safety regulations?

What's the correct procedure?

You must wear ear/eye protection.

This is a hazardous material.

What protective equipment should I wear?

You're not allowed to smoke here.

1 a Have you ever travelled on board a ship, or been on a cruise? Talk about the experience.

b What do you know about cruise ships? What sort of facilities are there on board?

2 a Work with a partner. Read the brochure about the *Serena*, a large cruise ship. Write the correct headings above the paragraphs.

> Electrical supply   Entertainment
>
> Fitness facilities   Foreign exchange
>
> Laundry   Take it easy
>
> Television   Your room

---

1   *Take it easy*

You'll have all the time in the world to enjoy the view, and a cool drink, from one of Serena's many lounges, bars and sun decks.

2 ....

Why not start the day with a swim (there are three swimming pools to choose from), then jog around the deck on the ship's on-board running track (early birds can watch the sun rise from the ocean). Finish with a workout in the gym, have a quick sauna, then go for breakfast, knowing you've really earned that extra portion!

3 ....

We offer three classes of cabin: Voyager, Explorer (with sea view) and Crest (with balcony).
All classes are available in the following formats:
- Single cabin
- Double cabin (available with double bed or twin beds)
- Family cabin (double bed + bunk beds)

All cabins have a washbasin, shower and toilet. Crest Class suites have a bath.

4 ....

The Serena has music for every taste, and from every era, with regular live shows in the cabaret bar by the ship's own band, The Serenades. In our nightclub, Force 12, the dance floor rocks every night with top DJ, Jeggar Marvin.

5 ....

A full range of international satellite channels is available on board. Viewing is subject to a small additional charge. Please ask at reception.

6 ....

All sockets are US format. International adapters are available for purchase on the ship.

7 ....

A next-day service is available, for a small charge. Please note, this does not include dry cleaning.

8 ....

All major currencies are available, including those required for shore excursions. Please note that cash purchases cannot be made on board. Purchases are charged to your bill or credit card.

b Find words in the texts to complete 1–12.

1 a room where you can sit and relax = a _lounge_

2 a place to go for a drink = a _____

3 a place where you would find exercise bikes = a

_____

4 a small room with a very high temperature = a _____

5 a group of musicians = a _____

6 a place where music's played until late = a _____

7 a bedroom on a ship = a _____

8 for one person = _____

9 for two people = _____

10 an area outside a window, where you can sit = a _____

11 you stand under this to wash = a _____

12 where you plug in electrical appliances = a _____

13 needed if plugs and sockets are different = an _____

14 a service for washing dirty clothes = _____

15 changing currencies = _____ _____

c Vocabulary practice ···> Page 105, Exercise 5.

d Work with a partner. Can you guess which of the facilities below were on the Titanic in 1912?

- lounges and bars • a band • a gym
- a sauna • a nightclub • electric sockets
- electric lights • lifts • a swimming pool
- toilets in cabins

3 a ▶▶| 76 **Listen to three conversations at the information desk on the Serena. Answer the questions.**

Conversation 1

1 What's the gym called?

2 How many saunas are there on the ship?

Conversation 2

3 Why doesn't the TV in the man's room work?

4 How much does it cost for television?

Conversation 3

5 What does the woman want to book?

6 Why is it necessary to reserve seats?

b ▶▶| 77 **Listen and repeat the sentences from the conversations. Copy the intonation.**

1 Hello. I'd like some information about the gym.

2 Is it open to everyone? Can anyone go in?

3 I think there's a problem with the TV in my room.

4 Are there any tickets left?

5 And how much are they?

6 OK, so can I book two seats, please?

c Look at the transcripts for 3a on page 125. Practise the conversations with a partner. Change roles. Try again from memory.

4 Communication practice 33. Student A ···> Page 87. Student B ···> Page 93.

5 Talk to a partner. Would you like to go on a cruise? What would you do on board? Say what you'd like and what you wouldn't like about spending time on a ship.

USEFUL LANGUAGE

Can anyone use the gym? Is there a sauna in there?

I think there's a problem with the shower in my room.

Do you sell international adapters for electrical sockets?

I'd like some information about entertainment on board.

Is it free?

There's a small charge.

12 | Agendas

12.1 | Attending meetings

GRAMMAR · · · · · · · · · · Time clauses

VOCABULARY Meetings

1 **Talk about meetings.**

How often do you go to meetings?

What sort of meetings do you attend?

How much time do you spend in meetings?

2 **a** ▶▶ **78** **Listen to the discussion at the start of a meeting at CC Software. Answer the questions.**

1 Why can't John Gates come to the meeting?

2 What happened last week?

3 What's the aim of this meeting?

b **Can you fill in the gaps in these sentences from the meeting?**

> agenda   apologies   attend
> called   chair   circulated   hold
> item   minutes   take

1 ... John Gates can't make it. He sends his _apologies_ .

2 John's asked me to _____ the meeting, so I'm in the hot seat!

3 OK, first, has everyone got an _____ ? John told me copies were _____ on Monday.

4 I got the agenda, but I didn't get a copy of the _____ from the meeting last week.

5 ... you all met last week to talk about the conference. I didn't _____ . I wasn't here last week.

6 No, we didn't _____ a meeting. We didn't _____ minutes or anything ...

7 So, we've _____ this meeting to talk about the sales conference ...

8 So, let's look at the first _____ on the agenda ...

c ▶▶ **78** **Listen again and check your answers.**

d Vocabulary practice ···▷ Page 105, Exercise 1.

e ▶▶ **79** PRONUNCIATION **Listen and repeat the words. Are the underlined sounds the same or different?**

			the same	different
1	<u>a</u>t	<u>a</u>ttend	☐	✓
2	<u>i</u>t	<u>i</u>tem	☐	☐
3	<u>o</u>ld	h<u>o</u>ld	☐	☐
4	l<u>a</u>te	circul<u>a</u>te	☐	☐
5	l<u>o</u>g	apol<u>o</u>gies	☐	☐

f **Work with a partner. Say sentences that mean the same as 1–6. Use words from the box in 2b.**

1 What are we going to discuss in the meeting?
   What's on the agenda?

2 I sent the agenda to everyone last Friday.

3 I wasn't at the last meeting.

4 John's sorry but he can't come.

5 Why have they arranged a meeting?

6 Let's look at the first point on the agenda.

3 **a** ▶▶ **80** **Listen to four short discussions (a–d) from the meeting at CC Software. Match each one to an item (1–7) on the agenda. Write the numbers of the items in the boxes.**

Discussion a ☐   Discussion b ☐   Discussion c ☐   Discussion d ☐

Meeting Agenda Planning meeting for the sales conference
Date 25th May   **Time** 2.00 pm   **Location** CC Software HQ
Participants   Victoria Carr, Amelia Donovan, John Gates, George
                        Lands, Lucy Ben, Trevor Ray
Chairperson   ~~John Gates~~ *Victoria Carr*
Apologies   *John Gates*

Item
1   Conference theme
2   Group meetings: Agendas? Participants?
3   Presentations: Subjects? Presenters?
4   Social events: What? Where?
5   Location
6   Dates
7   Any other business

b ▶▶ **80** **Listen again. Underline the words you hear.**

a I/I'll call them as soon as we/we'll finish.

b So before we/we'll decide, I/I'll visit all three hotels.

c We don't/won't book until we/we'll get replies from the branches.

d I/I'll ask him when I/I'll speak to him tomorrow.

c **Look at the transcript for 3b on page 125 and check your answers.**

Time clauses

I**'ll call** you when I **get** to the station.
I**'ll phone** you as soon as I **arrive**.
We **won't start** before you **arrive**.
We**'ll wait** until everyone **is** here.

···▶ **Grammar reference 5.4.2**

d Grammar practice ···▶ **Page 105, Exercise 2.**

e **Work in pairs. Make sentences.**

I / phone you / when / I / get home .

I / write / report / before / I / leave work .

I / work / until / I / finish / job .

4 Communication practice 34 ···▶ **Page 87. Work in groups of three or four.**

5 **Work with a partner. In your opinion, what makes good meetings? Discuss these points.**

- the length of the meeting
- the time of day the meeting is held
- the number of people who attend
- what's on the agenda
- preparation
- how the meeting is chaired

USEFUL LANGUAGE

Where are we going to hold the meeting?
Who's going to chair the meeting?
Who's going to take the minutes?
I missed the last meeting.
Fred can't come. He sends his apologies.
The last item on the agenda is 'any other business'.
I'll circulate the minutes next Monday.

1 **a** **How often do you talk about discussions you had with other people? Think about:**

- taking and receiving telephone messages
- telling colleagues what was discussed in meetings they didn't attend
- giving feedback about discussions with customers or suppliers

b **Do you think the following opinion is true? Can you give examples of it?**

'It's easy to report the facts after a meeting. It's more difficult to report people's opinions or feelings – and this can be very important in business.'

2 **a** **Read the email and answer the questions.**

1 Why did Amelia phone Sam and Mai?
2 How successful were her discussions with them?
3 Why did she speak to Tom?
4 Did Tom tell her what she wanted to know?

To: Victoria Carr   **From:** Amelia Donovan
Subject: Chinese culture speakers

Hi Victoria,

I spoke to Sam Wu yesterday, and he agreed to be one of our 'culture speakers' at the conference. Unfortunately, he's reluctant to make a presentation. He said he was happy to answer questions in the group discussion, though. I also spoke to Mai Cheng. She's very keen to give a talk, which is obviously good news.

So I think, with the two of them, we can arrange a presentation followed by a Q&A session, or something like that. Mai is going to think of some ideas, and meet Sam next week, so they can discuss them. I told her we were happy for her and Sam to decide what to talk about.

I also called Tom about his 'surprise gifts' for the conference. He refused to say what they are! He's decided not to say anything until the last minute, but he has promised to tell me what they are a week before the conference. I don't know what he's planning but, knowing Tom, it'll be something 'different'!

Regards,

Amelia

Amelia Donovan

Sales Consultant – CC Software

---

b **Work with a partner. From the email, work out what Sam, Mai and Tom said to Amelia on the phone, before she wrote the email message. Circle the correct answer: a or b.**

1 **Sam:** (a) Yes, OK, I'll be a speaker.
   b I don't really want to be a speaker.

2 **Sam:** a I'd love to make a presentation.
   b I don't really want to make a presentation.

3 **Sam:** a I'll answer questions.
   b I don't really want to answer questions.

4 **Mai:** a I'd love to make a presentation.
   b I don't want to make a presentation.

5 **Tom:** a OK, I'll tell you what the gifts are.
   b No, I'm not telling you what they are!

6 **Tom:** a Wait until the conference!
   b I'll tell you a few days before the conference.

c **Now write the parts of the email that match your answers in 2b.**

1 *he agreed to be one of our 'culture speakers'*
2 _____
3 _____
4 _____
5 _____
6 _____

d **Vocabulary practice ···> Page 105, Exercise 3.**

e ▶▶ **81** PRONUNCIATION Listen and repeat. How does the final **-d** in the verbs change in the sentences?

1 agreed   He agreed_to help.
2 refused   They refused_to do it.
3 promised   She promised_to send it.

3 **a** ▶▶ **82** Listen to a phone call between Victoria Carr and George Lands. Answer the questions.

1 What information does Victoria need?
2 Does George have the information?
3 Where's George going next?
4 What's he doing this afternoon?

b ▶▶ **82** Listen again. Are these sentences true (T) or false (F)? Change the false sentences to make them true.

1 George said the documents were in the computer. `F`
2 He said he could send them by email. ☐
3 Victoria said she needed the documents today. ☐
4 George said he would send them after his meeting. ☐
5 He said he would be in the office this afternoon. ☐
6 Victoria said she would phone him later today. ☐

Reported speech

'**I'm** very busy.' › He said he **was** very busy.
'I **have** a copy.' › He said he **had** a copy.
'I **can** email it.' › He said he **could** email it.
'**I'll** send it.' › He said he **would** send it.

···› **Grammar reference 12**

---

c Grammar practice ···› Page 105, Exercise 4.

d Work in groups of three. Take it in turns to give a message to the person next to you. He/She says the message to the third student in the group. (Invent your own message or use one of these.)

'I have a copy of the agenda.'
'I can email the document later.'
'I'll send the email after lunch.'
'I don't have the minutes from the last meeting.'
'I can't make it to the meeting tomorrow.'
'I'll call later.'

e ▶▶ **83** Listen to Victoria phoning George later. Answer the questions.

1 What does Victoria say about the Darley Hotel?
2 What does she think about the hotel's quote?
3 What's George going to do tomorrow?
4 What's Victoria going to do now?

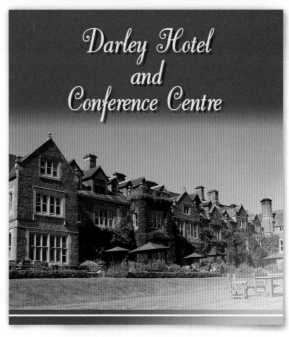

Darley Hotel and Conference Centre

f Work with a partner. Imagine you're Victoria Carr and your partner is John Gates. Tell your partner what you discussed on the phone with George Lands (in 3e). Change roles.

4 Communication practice 35. Student A ···› Page 88. Student B ···› Page 94.

USEFUL LANGUAGE

She promised to finish the report this week.

He agreed to increase the budget by 10%.

We've decided not to start work yet.

He said he was happy to attend and was keen to give a talk.

He doesn't like flying, so he was reluctant to go by plane.

They refused to do the work because it was too dangerous.

1 a Work with a partner. Write a list of things people do and say when they welcome visitors to their company.

b Can you give examples of how people from different countries welcome visitors?

2 a ▶▶ 84 Listen to four short conversations with a visitor, in a company. Match them to the photos (a–d). Write 1–4 in the boxes.

1 ☐   2 ☐   3 ☐   4 ☐

b Work with a partner. Look at the transcript for 2a on page 126. Find sentences from the conversations to match 1–9.

1 Apologising for not arriving on time
   Sorry I'm late.

2 Inviting someone to go through a door before you

3 Saying someone will come to meet you soon

4 Inviting someone to sit down

5 Asking if it's OK to open the window

6 Suggesting a break

7 Offering to take someone's coat

8 Giving something to someone

9 Offering someone a drink

c ▶▶ 84 Listen again. Now write the replies to the sentences in 2b.

1 *That's OK.*   6 ....

2 .... 7 ....

3 .... 8 ....

4 .... 9 ....

5 ....

d Vocabulary practice ···▸ Page 105, Exercise 5.

e Work with a partner. Practise welcoming each other.

3 a When people meet, they often make 'small talk'. What does 'small talk' mean?

b Work with a partner. Make a list of popular subjects of small talk. Suggest reasons why they're popular.

c ▶▶ 85 Listen to Amelia and Tom's conversation in the company cafeteria. What two subjects do they discuss as small talk?

d **Read the article and answer the questions. Use a dictionary to help you.**

1 What does the article say about small talk in international business?

2 What's 'cross-cultural' training?

3 What does the article suggest instead of small talk?

4 Are 'company lollipops' a joke or a serious idea?

e **What would your clients or colleagues think if you offered them a 'company lollipop'?**

f ▶▶ 86 **Listen to Tom and Amelia talking about company lollipops. Complete the expressions Amelia uses to show interest during the conversation.**

1 **Tom** They're gifts ... for the conference.

   Amelia ....!

2 **Tom** I give them to all my customers.

   Amelia ....?

3 **Tom** They're quite popular in the States ... as business gifts.

   Amelia ....?

4 **Tom** I just bought them.

   Amelia ....

g **Look at the transcript for 3f on page 127. Practise saying the conversation in pairs. Change roles.**

4 Communication practice 36 ···>
Page 88.

LINDA'S LOLLIES ®

Small talk can be all or nothing in international business. Sometimes, cultural differences are an interesting topic of conversation. Sometimes, they're a barrier. There's a growing market for 'cross-cultural' training, where businesspeople are taught what to do and say (and what *not* to do and say) when they meet people from different parts of the world. There's a lot to learn. There is, however, a much simpler solution. To avoid problems with small talk, you can simply avoid small talk altogether. How? Give your client or colleague a lollipop to suck!

If you think lollies are just for children, think again. Lollipops are popular business gifts in the USA, Canada, and also in Japan. The idea of producing 'gourmet lollies' for adults came from Linda Harkavy. Today, her New York based company, Linda's Lollies, sells a range of 'main course', 'dessert' and 'after dinner' lollipops, in flavours such as red hot spices, cherry cheesecake and cappuccino. Of course, the aim of 'company lollipops' isn't to stop the conversation. In fact, they're more likely to get everyone talking – businesspeople from most countries would be pretty surprised if they were given a lolly during a coffee break or presentation.

5 **What topics are suitable / not suitable for small talk in your country? Work in groups. Write a list of things you would/wouldn't talk about with colleagues from other countries.**

USEFUL LANGUAGE
Have a seat. Mr. Johnson will be with you in a moment.
Sorry I'm late.
That's OK.
My office is through here. After you.
Shall I take your coat?
Thanks. Here you are.
Do you mind if I open the window?
No, not at all.
Shall we take a break?
Yes, good idea.
Can I get you anything to drink?
No, I'm fine thanks.

Communication practice

Student A

You are on a training course. Introduce yourself to your partner, who is also on the course. Talk about your company and your job.

Your company: Context Interiors

Product/Service: design and manufacture of wallpaper

Your department: design

Your job title: design manager

Your team: 4 designers

Your responsibilities:

- manage the design team
- design new products
- do market research on competitors' products

Your boss: product development manager

Now listen to your partner. Ask questions and make notes about his/her job and company.

Student A

You are a representative at a trade fair. Your partner wants to know about your products and services. Use the information to talk about your company and answer your partner's questions.

Your company: MaxVid

Your product:

- big TV screens (for pop concerts, sports events, amusement parks, trade fairs, etc.)
- four screens: 3, 5, 10 and 15 metres wide
- for indoor and outdoor use

Your services:

- design and manufacture of screens
- available to buy or rent
- engineers install and operate screens if you rent
- international after-sales service

Now you are the managing director of a chain of hotels. Your partner is a representative for Floral World at a trade fair. Find out more about Floral World's products and services. In particular, you are interested in information about Japanese-style flower displays for a conference.

Practise ordering a meal in a restaurant. Take it in turns to be the customer and the waiter/waitress.

Customer: You arrive at the restaurant. You have a reservation. Look at the menu and order. After the meal, ask for the bill and pay.

Waiter/Waitress: Welcome the customer and show him/her to a table. Give him/her a menu and take the order. During the meal, check that everything is OK. Finally bring the bill.

Menu for £18

Starters
Chicken and leek soup
Tomato soup with cream
Mixed salad

Main courses
Grilled salmon with rice and broccoli
Roast beef with roast potatoes and a selection of fresh vegetables
Vegetarian salad with cheddar cheese
Grilled steak with chips and peas
Roast lamb with mashed potato and carrots

Desserts
Apple pie with fresh cream
Strawberry ice cream
Fruit salad

Drinks (extra)

Mineral water (still or sparkling)	bottle - £3.50
	glass - £1.00
Fruit juice (orange, apple, tomato)	glass - £1.50

Student A

You are a managing director. Your company is moving to new offices this week. Telephone the office manager (Student B), to get an update. Ask questions and make notes of the answers.

A Are the technicians installing the computers?
B Yes, but they're one day behind schedule.

Start the call. Say who you are and ask about the schedule.

technicians / install computers ?

workers / paint reception ?

electricians / work on the fourth floor ?

engineers / check telephone lines ?

photocopier / work ?

move / go well ?

Now change roles.

COMMUNICATION PRACTICE 5
(2.2, EXERCISE 3)

Read the job advert. With your partner, decide which skills, personal characteristics and experience are most important for the job.

Head of sales and marketing

Who are we?
I-train.com produces online management training material for companies worldwide. Companies pay to access the training programmes on our website.

Who are we looking for?
We need an experienced and dynamic person (28–45) to lead our sales and marketing department.

About the job
- Managing a team of 20 telephone sales staff and 10 marketing assistants.
- Planning a new sales and marketing strategy for Asia.
- Working with important customers in Japan and China.
- Salary depends on skills and experience. (£45,000–£65,000)

Skills and experience
- management experience
- experience in sales and marketing training
- strong IT skills
- good communication skills in English. Other foreign languages an advantage, especially Japanese or Chinese.

For further information and to apply online please visit www.I-train.com (ref. AA01)

Now read the human resources manager's notes about two people the company wants to interview for the job. Discuss the strengths and weaknesses of each and decide who is the best person for the job. Give your reasons why.

ITrain.co.uk
Interview Notes

Job *Head of sales and marketing*
Name Jessie Lin
Nationality Chinese
Age 37
Present post and salary sales manager (£50,000)
Skills and experience
* Masters degree (Marketing)
* leads team of 4
* good contacts with Chinese customers
* very good sales experience (IT software)
* fluent Chinese and very good English

ITrain.co.uk
Interview Notes

Job *Head of sales and marketing*
Name Eric Terrett
Nationality French
Age 50
Present post and salary
marketing and sales manager (£60,000)
Skills and experience
* MBA (Harvard)
* 12 years manager of a big team of sales and marketing staff in international company
* regular contacts with customers in China
* 3 years in Korea as sales manager for IT company
* 4 years training manager for an IT company in Kyoto
* native speaker of French, good English and Japanese
* looking for a new experience and challenge

COMMUNICATION PRACTICE 6
(2.3, EXERCISE 3)

Discuss your interests with your partner. Try to find five things that you have in common. Then change partners.

A   I like football, but I'm not very good at it
B   Me too – I like watching football, but I'm hopeless at playing!

Make a list of what you have in common so that you can report back to the class.

We both like football, but we're not very good at playing.

COMMUNICATION PRACTICE 7
(3.1, EXERCISE 4)

You need to buy new carpets for your offices. Compare the quotes in the chart with your partner. Decide which quote to accept.

Quality Carpets has a better delivery time than Minster Weave, but …

	Melton Carpets	Minster Weave	Quality Carpets
delivery time	21 days (express delivery in 4 days = £300)	10 days	5 days
delivery charge	over 500 m² = free	over 500 m² = £20	free
quality and price	high quality = £24	high quality = £28	high quality = £30 top quality = £40
discount	over 500 m² = 20%	over 500 m² = 15%	over 500 m² = 30%
fitting charge	over 500 m² = free	free	over 500 m² = £150

COMMUNICATION PRACTICE 8
(3.2, EXERCISE 4)

You and your partner are in charge of finding and designing a new office space for your company. Look at the list of possible facilities and put them in order of importance (1 = most important, 10 = least important).

A   I think a nice reception area is the most important thing. It's important to impress clients and visitors.
B   I don't agree …

☐ lift
☐ reception area
☐ meeting rooms
☐ kitchen
☐ coffee area
☐ parking
☐ water machine
☐ air conditioning
☐ windows
☐ restaurant

COMMUNICATION PRACTICE 9
(3.3, EXERCISE 4)

You are visiting your partner's country on business, then you are taking a week's holiday to see some of the country. Ask your partner to recommend three interesting places. Ask questions and decide which place you'd most like to visit.

What's it like in …?
What's the best time of year to visit …?
What's the weather like in …?
Can you recommend …?

Now change roles.

COMMUNICATION PRACTICE 10
(4.1, EXERCISE 3)

Student A

Last year, these two products were complete flops. Look at product A and guess why it was a flop. Comment on the name, size, screen, weight, price, battery life and colour of the product. Explain your ideas using *too/enough*. Your partner will tell you if you're right or not.

Product A

Special Offer on Big Boy Laptops
Good battery (30 minutes)
10% off. Only $3899.
Available colour: pink.

Product B

Test drive a Nogo!
Top speed 40 kph.
100km / 20 litres.
One year's free membership of the 3-wheelers' club.
Price £23,500.
Available colour: pea green.

Now listen to your partner guess why Product B was a flop and make notes. Then use the information to explain why the product failed.

Your partner's ideas:

....
....
....

Why Product B flopped
Name of product: too negative / not positive enough
Size: too short / too high
Top speed: not fast enough
Design: too dangerous / not safe enough
Price: too expensive
Petrol: not economical enough
Colour: too horrible

COMMUNICATION PRACTICE 11
(4.2, EXERCISE 4)

Student A

You are a human resources manager. You are interviewing Student B for a job. Ask your partner to talk about a project he/she worked on last year. If the project was not on schedule or not on budget, ask why not. Make notes of his/her replies.

project?
....

project details?
....

team?
....

on schedule?
....

problems?
....

solutions?
....

Now you are at an interview for a job, Student B is the interviewer. Answer his/her questions about a project you worked on last year. You want the job, so be positive and enthusiastic!

Project:
advert for machine

Project details:
visit factory / speak to marketing manager / discuss competition / agree budget / take photographs / discuss sample advert with manager / make changes / deliver final advert

Team:
leader / team of 4

Schedule:
6 months (actual time = 4 months)

Difficulties/problems:
no big problems / first photographs not good enough

Solutions:
visit factory again / use different camera

COMMUNICATION PRACTICE 12
(4.3, EXERCISE 4)

Discuss with your partner what you did last weekend, or what you normally do at the weekend. Try to find five things that you both did/normally do.

A   I normally have a lie in on Sundays.

B   Me too, but last Sunday I got up early to do some work on the house.

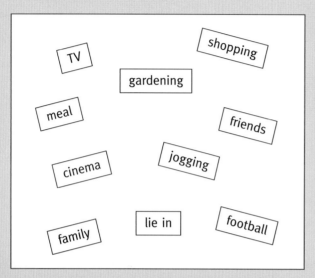

COMMUNICATION PRACTICE 13
(5.1, EXERCISE 4)

Student A

You are having a meeting with your partner to discuss a presentation you are giving in Barcelona next month. Look at the list of action points and agree to do all the jobs between you. You are a good communicator and work fast, so offer to do the things you do best.

Shall I ...?   I'll ... .

Action points – Barcelona presentation

- Find out sales figures for the presentation.
- Talk to design department about photos for the presentation.
- Write the presentation.
- Show the presentation to your boss (you don't want to do this!).
- Book flights to Barcelona.
- Book hotel in Barcelona.

COMMUNICATION PRACTICE 14
(5.2, EXERCISE 5)

Student A

You are the sales manager of IT Control Systems. You want to visit a company called Santik to present your new software for stock control. Telephone the sales manager of Santik (Student B), and make arrangements for the visit. Make notes of what you agree.

Start the call.

- Introduce yourself.
- Talk about the new product.
- Ask to visit to do a presentation. You need to meet the sales manager.
- Arrange a day and a time for next week. You aren't free on Wednesdays or Thursdays.

Now work together to write an email from the sales manager. Confirm the arrangements you made on the telephone.

COMMUNICATION PRACTICE 15
(5.3, EXERCISE 3)

Student A

You are a tourist visiting Cambridge. Student B works in the tourist information office. Ask for the following information. Make notes.

List of hotels (not too expensive):

Map of the city centre – how much?:

Information about the city's history:

Most interesting places to visit:

Now you work in the tourist information office and your partner is a tourist. However, today you are very tired and very busy, and as a result you aren't very helpful. You are also new to the job and you don't know Cambridge very well. Use the following information.

No lists of restaurants. No good fish restaurants. Good hotdogs near station.

Maps – no map of city centre.
Map of England – £5.50.

Opening hours – you don't know.

Best place for souvenirs – the airport.

COMMUNICATION PRACTICE 16
(6.1, EXERCISE 3)

Look at the list of ideas for new tourist activities. Take it in turns to make predictions about the ideas. Student A starts and makes a positive or negative prediction. Student B disagrees and makes a different prediction.

A   I think lots of people will go to these hotels – it's very exciting!

B   I don't agree. People won't want to stay in places as dangerous as that.

1   A hotel chain wants to build 5-star hotels near famous volcanoes.
2   A travel company wants to offer 30-day tours to the Arctic Circle.
3   A travel company wants to offer skiing tours on Mount Everest.
4   A construction company is going to build a tropical dome in the south of Spain.
5   A travel agent wants to offer beach holidays in the north of Europe.
6   A tour company for the over 50s wants to offer guided tours of the great libraries of Europe.
7   A British fast food restaurant company wants to offer 'gastronomic tourism' in the UK.

Look at the list again. Decide how probable it is that ideas will be successful. Use *certainly*, *maybe*, *probably*, *definitely*, *possibly* and *perhaps*.

COMMUNICATION PRACTICE 17
(6.2, EXERCISE 3)

You are and your partner are hoping to start your own business. Here are some notes from your business plan. Read them through carefully.

Online training programmes – management training, team building etc.

Lessons by email, phone or video conference

Profit forecast: £130,000 – year 1, £190,000 0 – year 2, £350,000 – year 3

Staff needs: 20 permanent trainers, office manager, secretary, marketing consultant

Office needs: small office, no need for city centre location

Advertising campaign: in national newspapers

Now discuss what you'll do if these things happen:

If people don't like video conferencing, we'll offer courses in a classroom.

- If people don't like video conferencing?
- If there are problems with the Internet (conection, viruses etc.)?
- If your profit forecasts for year 1 are too high?
- If you can't find enough permanent trainers?
- If you can only find expensive office space in the city centre?
- If it's too expensive to advertise in national newspapers?

Now compare your decisions with another pair of students. Did you have the same solutions to the problems?

COMMUNICATION PRACTICE 18
(6.3, EXERCISE 4)

Student A

You want to book a flight to Faro, in Portugal, leaving on Monday 16th May and returning on Tuesday 26th May. Student B works for the airline. Find out the following information and book the seat using your credit card.

- Flight times
- Baggage allowance
- Price including taxes
- Excess baggage charge

Now change roles. Student B wants to buy a ticket. Answer his/her questions and take the booking.

Destination: Madrid, Spain
Outbound flights: Tuesday, Friday 9.00 and 19.45
Return flights: Tuesday, Friday 10.00 and 20.30
Prices:
    Tuesday €60 one-way
    Friday €95 one-way
    evening flights €10 extra
    10% discount on Tuesday flights next week
Baggage allowance: 20kg
Excess baggage charge: €10 per kilo

COMMUNICATION PRACTICE 19
(7.1, EXERCISE 4)

Student A

You are starting a new job today. You are meeting the training manager to decide what your training needs are for the year. The training manager (your partner) will ask you if you've used the following programmes before. Use the information in the chart to answer.

B   Have you used FastNotes email system before?
A   Yes, I have. I used the same system ... .

Programme	Experienced user?
FastNotes email system	✓ use / same system / in last company
FileShare database	✗ not / work / with databases / in last job
Excel	✗ not / use / Excel / in last job
Word	✓ use / a lot / in last job
PowerPoint	✓ work with / PowerPoint / a little / in last job

Now change roles. Ask your partner if he/she has used the programmes in the chart before. Make a note of his/her replies so that you can plan the training programme.

A   Have you used FastNotes email system before?
B   No, I haven't. I used FastMail ... .

COMMUNICATION PRACTICE 20
(7.2, EXERCISE 6)

Student A

You are Student B's boss. He/She is in Poland to consider the possibility of opening a new office there. He/she calls to give you an update. Ask questions to find out more information. Make notes of the answers.

1   meet / local property consultant yet ?
2   look at / possible locations for office yet ?
3   plan / budget for new office yet ?
4   meet / local recruitment consultant yet ?
5   write report / on state of Polish economy ?

Now change roles.

COMMUNICATION PRACTICE 21
(7.3, EXERCISE 4)

Take it in turns to ask and answer questions, using the list. Describe the experience and how you felt.

A   Have you ever stayed in a 5-star hotel?
B   Yes I have. I stayed in the Hotel Claris in Barcelona. It was fantastic but very expensive!

Have you ever ...
    fly / in a hot-air balloon ?
    swim / in the sea at night ?
    drive / a sports car ?
    run / a marathon ?
    win / a prize or competition ?
    eat / in a very expensive restaurant ?
    meet / a famous person ?
    travel / somewhere dangerous ?
    stay / in a 5-star hotel ?

COMMUNICATION PRACTICE 22
(8.1, EXERCISE 4)

Student A

Look at the information about your company's performance so far this year. Explain the information to your partner.

Rite-clean company performance Quarters 1 & 2	
Production	▲ 8%
Sales	▼ 5%
Costs:	
salaries/bonuses	▼ 3%
staff travel	▲ 11%
pension payments	▲ 3%
Profits	▼ 11%

Now listen your partner and complete the information about his/her company.

CopyLite company performance Quarter 1	▲	▼	
Production	☐	☐	...... %
Sales	☐	☐	...... %
Costs:			
salaries/bonuses	☐	☐	...... %
staff travel	☐	☐	...... %
pension payments	☐	☐	...... %
Profits	☐	☐	...... %

COMMUNICATION PRACTICE 23
(8.2, EXERCISE 4)

Student A

Look at the information about property prices in London. Answer your partner's questions.

Average price: 2-bedroom apartment in London	
1990	£60,000
1994	£40,000
1996	£70,000
1999	£100,000
2002	£180,000
2006	£240,000
2012	£480,000?

Now ask your partner about property prices in Liverpool. Use the correct tense for the questions.

what / cost / a house in 1990 ?
what / happen / in 1994 ?
what / happen / in the last ten years ?
what / cost / a house now ?
what / cost / a house in 2012 ?

COMMUNICATION PRACTICE 24
(8.3, EXERCISE 5)

Discuss what you watched on TV last night/week and the type of programmes you like watching. Try to find as many things as possible that you both like/dislike.

A   I watched that new quiz show last night, on Channel 5. Did you see it?

B   No, I watched a documentary about ... and the news. I don't really like / But I like quiz shows. Did you see ...?

COMMUNICATION PRACTICE 25
(9.1, EXERCISE 4)

Student A

Listen to your partner describe a new business concept. Ask questions for more information. Take notes and be prepared to explain the concept to another student.

You have a new idea for a way of selling CDs (music and films) online. Read the description of your business concept, then use the passive to describe it to your partner.

OK, this is my new business plan. First, CDs are ordered through the website ...

- Customers order CDs through the website.
- People send the CDs back to us when they've finished.
- We pay the postage.
- We give the customer a 50% discount off his/her next purchase.
- We sell the second-hand CDs for an even bigger discount.

COMMUNICATION PRACTICE 26
(9.2, EXERCISE 3)

You and your partner are management consultants. A company has come to you for advice about expanding their business. First, read the description of the company:

The Flying Duck

Restaurant with 30 tables – 100 seats

New menu every month

10 staff

Annual costs:
  rent – £0
  (they own the building)
  staff – £150,000
  food/drink – £300,000

Profit last year: £50,000

The Flying Duck's objective is to double its annual profit. Make a list of recommendations for the restaurant's management. Consider the following:

- costs
- staff
- expanding business
- investment
- risks
- advertising/marketing

Firstly, we think you need to cut costs – you could ... .

Now work with another pair of students. Imagine that they are the restaurant owners. Explain your strategy to them. Then change roles.

COMMUNICATION PRACTICE 27
(9.3, EXERCISE 3)

Make a note of your favourite:

- search engine
- news website
- shopping website
- banking website

Ask your partner about his/her favourite sites. Do you use any of the same sites? Find out more information about your partner's favourites. Ask questions.

need / register ?

need / password ?

you / a member ?

how much / cost / membership ?

secure ?

COMMUNICATION PRACTICE 28
(10.1, EXERCISE 4)

You work for SunSol, a sunglasses company based in California. You manufacture sunglasses at your factory near San Francisco and sell glasses to the US market. Sales are down this year, and you need to cut costs, improve sales and increase profits by the end of the year. Discuss these areas with your partner and make suggestions.

A   OK, I've got an idea. How about ...?
B   That's an interesting idea, but what about ...?
- production costs in the US
- new products
- new markets
- marketing/advertising
- price
- discounts

Now compare your suggestions with another pair.

COMMUNICATION PRACTICE 29
(10.2, EXERCISE 3)

You work at the head office of BEC, a large international company. Your manager has asked you and your colleagues to think of ways to reduce costs at the head office. Costs include paper, electricity bills, telephone bills, drinking water, etc.

Have a meeting with your colleagues. Working together, think of ideas, develop them and make a list of proposals for your manager. Use the Six Thinking Hats to work through the stages:

Step 1 – White Hat: Discuss only the facts

Step 2 – Green Hat: Make suggestions

Step 3 – Red Hat: Give first reactions to suggestions

Step 4 – Yellow Hat: Discuss the advantages of suggestions

Step 5 – Black Hat: Discuss the disadvantages of suggestions

(Step 6 – Blue Hat: Manage the discussion)

Before you start, you should choose one person to chair the meeting. He/She should occasionally put on the blue hat to manage the discussion and help to decide what proposals you will present.

COMMUNICATION PRACTICE 30
(10.3, EXERCISE 5)

Student A

You're travelling from Cambridge to Paris via London. Your train from Cambridge was delayed and you've missed your Eurostar connection. You have a return seat in Standard Class. Speak to a Eurostar representative (Student B) at Waterloo Station.

- Explain the situation.
- Find out:
  when the next train is (your meeting in Paris starts at 15.00).
  if your ticket is valid for other trains.
  if you have to pay a supplement.
- Thank the person for his/her help.

Now change roles.

COMMUNICATION PRACTICE 31
(11.1, EXERCISE 3)

Student A

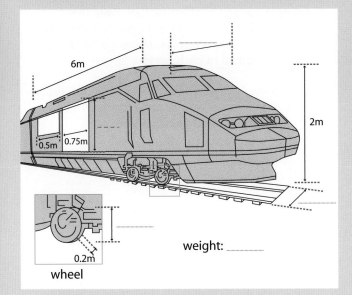

wheel

Look at the diagram of a high speed train.
Ask your partner for the missing dimensions.

How wide/long/high/heavy ...?

Now answer your partner's questions about the diagram.

It's ... wide/long.   The weight/height is ... .

COMMUNICATION PRACTICE 32
(11.2, EXERCISE 4)

You and your partner work in the health and safety department at Frisky Frozen Fish Fingers. Your company always gives new factory workers health and safety training. All workers must pass a test called 'Safety in Food Factories – Common Sense'.

To help them write the test, the human resources department have asked you to make a list of obvious food safety precautions that people should know. With your partner, make a list of things that people must and mustn't do when they work in a food factory.

You must wear gloves if you work with food. You musn't ... .

When you've finished, compare your suggestions with another pair.

COMMUNICATION PRACTICE 33
(11.3, EXERCISE 4)

Student A

You are a customer on the cruise ship *Serena*. Student B is the receptionist. Role play the following situations.

1 You want more information about the ship's bar and restaurant. You are a vegetarian.

2 Your mobile phone charger doesn't work. You bought it in France.

3 You want to find out about live music on the ship. Buy two tickets for something you're interested in.

Now change roles.

COMMUNICATION PRACTICE 34
(12.1, EXERCISE 4)

You're having a meeting to plan what you need to do for your sales conference. Choose one person to be the chair. The chair should:

* announce apologies
* check everyone has an agenda/the minutes from the last meeting
* confirm the time/place of the next meeting

Look at the list of jobs and decide who will do what and when. Organise the jobs into a logical order.

Agenda – Sales conference planning meeting
Date: 1st June Time: 2 pm Location: Meeting room 1
Participants: ....
Chair: ....
Apologies: Vicky Abbott

Agenda items
Jobs to do before the conference:

* Write presentations
* Circulate conference programme to all staff
* Decide dates for conference
* Decide who's going to give presentations
* Choose hotel/restaurants
* Practise presentations
* Write agenda for sales conference meetings
* Choose chair for sales conference meetings
* Plan social events

Next meeting: 8th June, 2 pm. Meeting room 1.

Student A

You attended a meeting yesterday about organising your company's annual sales conference, but you were delayed and missed the first three items on the agenda. Ask your partner to tell you what was discussed. Make notes.

Meeting Agenda
Planning meeting for the sales conference

Date 25th May **Time** 2.00 pm
Location Meeting Room 2

Participants: Sally Smith, Clare Wilkins, Chris O'Neil

Item

1 Conference theme

2 Group meetings: Agendas? Participants?

3 Presentations: Subjects? Presenters?

4 Social events: What? Where? *Chris – prefers a big conference dinner for all employees. Sally agrees. Clare – keen to have lots of smaller events – theatre, bowling etc.*

5 Location *Clare – reluctant to go abroad – too expensive. Sally and Chris – we have enough budget.*

6 Dates *Sally will speak to the branches to find out best dates.*

7 Any other business *Clare will chair the next meeting.*

Now tell your partner what was discussed after item 3 of the meeting. Use the agenda to help you.

We discussed / agreed to ... . Chris/Clare/Sally said ...

Make small talk with other students. Show interest during the conversation. Keep the conversation going as long as you can, then move on to talk to someone else. Make a note of how long you talked to each person.

Now make a list of the subjects you talked about. Compare them with other students' conversations. Who had the longest conversation?

Student B

You are on a training course. Listen to your partner, who is also on the course. Ask questions and make notes about his/her job and company.

Now introduce yourself to your partner. Talk about your company and your job.

Your company: TD Consulting
Product/Service: management consulting
Your department: export consulting
Your job title: export consultant
Your team: 1 personal assistant, 2 export assistants
Your responsibilities:
- manage the team
- visit important clients
- work with foreign agencies

Your boss: senior export consultant

COMMUNICATION PRACTICE 2
(1.2, EXERCISE 4)

Student B

You are a pop concert and sports event organiser. Student A is a representative for MaxVid at a trade fair. Find out more about MaxVid's products and services. In particular, you are interested in information about a 20 metre-wide screen for use outdoors.

Now you are a representative at a trade fair. Student A is the managing director of a chain of hotels. He/She wants to know about your products and services. Use the information to talk about your company and answer questions.

Your company: Floral World

Your product:

- silk flower displays for hotels and conference centres
- displays in modern, traditional or Japanese style

Your services:

- individual design of displays
- creative experts to advise clients
- The displays are for all public areas (receptions, restaurants, meeting and conference rooms etc.)

COMMUNICATION PRACTICE 4
(2.1, EXERCISE 4)

Student B

You are an office manager. Your company is moving to new offices this week and you are organising the move. Your managing director (Student A) telephones you for an update on the schedule. Answer his/her questions using the following information.

> *Office move update – some problems, but generally on schedule.*
>
> | Job | Schedule |
> |---|---|
> | installing computers | 1 day behind |
> | painting reception | 2 days ahead – now painting meeting room |
> | electrics on fourth floor | 1 day late – working on third floor |
> | telephone lines | checked, but phones not working |
> | photocopier | problems with socket |

Now change roles.

COMMUNICATION PRACTICE 10
(4.1, EXERCISE 3)

Student B

Last year, these two products were complete flops. Listen to your partner guess why Product A was a flop and make notes. Then use the information to explain why the product failed.

Product A

Special Offer on Big Boy Laptops
Good battery
(30 minutes)
10% off. Only $3899.
Available colour: pink.

Product B

Test drive a Nogo!
Top speed 40 kph.
100km / 20 litres.
One year's free membership of the 3-wheelers' club.
Price £23,500.
Available colour: pea green.

Your partner's ideas:

....

....

....

Why Product A flopped

Name of product: not serious/professional enough

Size: too long / too wide

Screen: not big enough

Weight: too heavy / not light enough

Price: not cheap enough / too expensive

Battery: not long enough

Colour: too horrible

Now look at Product B and guess why it was a flop. Comment on the name, size, top speed, design, price, petrol consumption and colour of the product. Explain your ideas using *too/enough*. Your partner will tell you if you're right or not.

COMMUNICATION PRACTICE 11
(4.2, EXERCISE 4)

Student B

You are at an interview for a job and Student A is the interviewer. Answer his/her questions about a project you worked on last year. You want the job, so be positive and enthusiastic!

Project:

web page for company

Project details:

visit company / find out needs / discuss budget / take photographs in offices / produce sample web page / discuss sample with manager / make changes / deliver final product

Team:

leader / team of 3

Schedule:

10 months (actual time = 1 year)

Difficulties/problems:

budget too small / one member of team – new job

Solutions:

negotiate bigger budget / appoint new colleague

Now you are a human resources manager. You are interviewing Student A for a job. Ask him/her to talk about a project he/she worked on last year. If the project was not on schedule or not on budget, ask why not. Make notes of his/her replies.

project?
project details?
team?
on schedule?
difficulties/problems?
solutions?

COMMUNICATION PRACTICE 13
(5.1, EXERCISE 4)

Student B

You are having a meeting with your partner to discuss a presentation you are giving in Barcelona next month. Look at the list of action points and agree to do all the jobs between you. You're very busy at the moment, so offer to do two or three things which you know you can do quickly.

Shall I ...?   I'll ... .

Action points – Barcelona presentation

- Find out sales figures for the presentation.
- Talk to design department about photos for the presentation.
- Write the presentation.
- Show the presentation to your boss (you don't want to do this!).
- Book flights to Barcelona.
- Book hotel in Barcelona.

COMMUNICATION PRACTICE 14
(5.2, EXERCISE 5)

Student B

You are the manager of Santik. A sales manager from another company (Student A) telephones you. He/She wants to visit your company. Use the following questions and information in the conversation. Make notes of what you agree.

- Name of company?
- What new product do they have?
- You're not in office next week.
- Warehouse manager is free – OK?
- Agree a day (not Mondays or Tuesdays).
- Agree a time (not before lunch).

Now work together to write an email from the sales manager. Confirm the arrangements you made on the telephone.

COMMUNICATION PRACTICE 15
(5.3, EXERCISE 3)

Student B

You work in a tourist information office and your partner is a tourist. You like your job and you're very helpful and friendly. Answer your partner's questions, using the following information.

Hotels – list with all prices (hotels in old city centre expensive – cheaper near station).

Map – free.

History of Cambridge booklet – £4.50. Very good value. Lots of nice photos.

Places to visit? Museum (guided tour at 2 pm and 4 pm).

Now you are a tourist and Student A works in a tourist information office. Ask for the following information. Make notes.

List of restaurants (you like fish):

Map of the city centre:

Museum opening hours:

Best place for souvenirs:

COMMUNICATION PRACTICE 18
(6.3, EXERCISE 4)

Student B

You work for GlenAir. Student A wants to buy a ticket. Answer his/her questions and take the booking.

Destination: Faro, Portugal
Outbound flights: Monday, Friday 10.00 and 17.30
Return flights: Monday, Wednesday, Friday 11.00 and 16:45
Prices:
Monday €50 one-way
Friday €75 one-way
Baggage allowance: 20kg
Excess baggage charge: €10 per kilo

Now you're the customer. You want to book a flight to Madrid sometime next week. Student B works for the airline. Find out the following information and book the seat using your credit card.

- Flight times
- Baggage allowance
- Price including taxes
- Excess baggage charge

COMMUNICATION PRACTICE 19
(7.1, EXERCISE 4)

Student B

You are a training manager. Your partner is starting work at your company today and you need to find out about his/her training needs. Ask if he/she has used the following programmes before, and make a note of his/her replies.

FastNotes email system, FileShare database, Excel, Word, PowerPoint

B Have you used FastNotes email system before?
A Yes, I have. I used the same system ... .

Now change roles. The training manager will ask you if you've used the same programmes before. Use the information in the chart to answer.

Programme	Experienced user?
FastNotes email system	✗ use / FastMail / in last company
FileShare database	✓ work / with FileShare / in last job
Excel	✓ use / Excel / in last job
Word	✗ not use / in last job
PowerPoint	✗ not write / presentations / in last job

COMMUNICATION PRACTICE 20
(7.2, EXERCISE 6)

Student B

You are on a visit to Poland. Your company is thinking about opening a new office in Krakow. Look at your 'to do' list. Phone your boss in the UK (Student A) to give an update on your progress.

Poland visit – to do

1 Meet local property consultant Done.
2 Look at possible locations for office
   Seen two possible locations.
3 Plan budget for new office
   Done, but problems here. Budget is too small.
4 Meet local recruitment consultant
   Not done. Difficult to find local recruitment experts.
5 Write report on Polish economic situation
   Not done. No time.

Now change roles.

COMMUNICATION PRACTICE 22
(8.1, EXERCISE 4)

Student B

Listen to your partner describe his/her company's performance so far this year. Complete the information.

Rite-clean company performance Quarters 1 & 2

	▲	▼	
Production	☐	☐	.... %
Sales	☐	☐	.... %
Costs:			
salaries/bonuses	☐	☐	.... %
staff travel	☐	☐	.... %
pension payments	☐	☐	.... %
Profits	☐	☐	.... %

Now look at the information about your company's performance so far this year. Explain the information to your partner.

CopyLite company performance Quarter 1

Production	▲ 3%
Sales	▲ 25%
Costs:	
salaries/bonuses	▲ 10%
staff travel	▼ 7%
pension payments	▼ 11%
Profits	▲ 15%

COMMUNICATION PRACTICE 23
(8.2, EXERCISE 4)

Student B

Ask your partner about property prices in London. Use the correct tense for the questions.

what / cost / an apartment in 1990 ?

what / happen / in 1994 ?

what / happen / in the last ten years ?

what / cost / an apartment now ?

what / cost / an apartment in 2012 ?

Now look at the information about property prices in Liverpool. Answer your partner's questions.

Average price: 2-bedroom house in Liverpool

1990	£40,000
1994	£30,000
1996	£50,000
1999	£90,000
2002	£95,000
2006	£100,000
2012	£200,000?

COMMUNICATION PRACTICE 25
(9.1, EXERCISE 4)

Student B

You have a new idea for teaching English online. Read the description of the business concept then use the passive to describe it to your partner.

OK, this is my new business plan. Firstly, classes are taken using a webcam ...

- Students take classes, using a webcam on the Internet.
- Students practise speaking with the microphone.
- Students send homework to the teacher by email.
- The teacher checks homework and returns it by email.
- The teacher uses interesting websites as part of the lesson.
- The teacher gives students a certificate at the end of the course.

Now listen to your partner describe a new business concept. Ask questions for more information. Take notes so that you can explain the concept later to another student.

COMMUNICATION PRACTICE 30
(10.3, EXERCISE 5)

Student B

You are a Eurostar representative at Waterloo Station in London. Listen to a passenger (Student A). Find out what type of ticket he/she has and answer his/her questions. Use the following information.

11.00 – arrives Paris 14.30. (only First Class seats available)

12.00 – arrives Paris 15.30 (Standard and First Class seats available)

Cost of an upgrade to First Class: £100 (return)

Tickets are valid on all trains.

Now change roles.

COMMUNICATION PRACTICE 31
(11.1, EXERCISE 3)

Student B

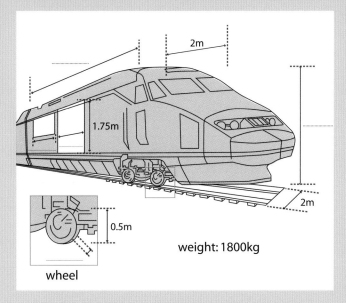

2m

1.75m

2m

0.5m

weight: 1800kg

wheel

Look at the diagram of a high-speed train. Answer your partner's questions about the diagram.

It's ... wide/long.   The weight/height is ... .

Now ask your partner for the missing dimensions.

How wide/long/high/heavy ...?

COMMUNICATION PRACTICE 33
(11.3, EXERCISE 4)

Student B

You are a receptionist on the cruise ship *Serena*. Student A is a passenger. Answer his/her questions for three different situations. Use the information.

Serena Bar and Restaurant

Restaurant open everyday 6–11 pm

Drinks served until midnight

Mediterranean cuisine

Vegetarian options

Fine wine list

Electrical supply

Electricity sockets are US format. Adapters $6.99.

Available from our shops.

Live music – *Wednesday 31st May*

Laguna Bar – The Easy Jazz Quartet. 8 pm. Free entry.

Cabaret Bar – The Serenades. 9 pm. Free entry. Booking required.

Force 12 disco – DJ Jeggar Martin. 10 pm. Entry $6.

Now change roles.

COMMUNICATION PRACTICE 35
(12.2, EXERCISE 4)

Student B

You attended a meeting yesterday about organising your company's annual sales conference. Your partner was delayed and missed the first three items on the agenda. Tell your partner what was discussed. Use the agenda to help you.

We discussed / agreed to … . Chris/Clare/Sally said … .

Meeting Agenda
Planning meeting for the sales conference

Date 25th May **Time** 2.00 pm
Location Meeting Room 2

Participants: Sally Smith, Clare Wilkins, Chris O'Neil

Item

1 Conference theme Sally wants 'Innovation' again. Clare prefers 'Learning from the past'. Chris – happy to let Sally and Clare decide.

2 Group meetings: Agendas? Participants? Chair – Chris. Chris will decide who to invite.

3 Presentations: Subjects? Presenters? Neil from Kuwait office doesn't want to present. Mark from Japan office is happy to give a presentation. Clare will help prepare the presentation.

4 Social events: What? Where?

5 Location

6 Dates

7 Any other business

You had to leave the meeting and missed items 4–7 on the agenda. Ask your partner to tell you what was discussed. Make notes.

Grammar and vocabulary practice

1 Find the words and fill in the gaps.

> brispolenes lead troper
> agmane grehac kool

1 He's _responsible_ for export sales.
2 I _____ five people.
3 I _____ to the office manager.
4 I'm in _____ of the London office.
5 They _____ with financial problems.
6 We _____ after customers in 50 countries.

2 Make positive and negative sentences.

1 I / be in charge .
   I'm in charge.
   I'm not in charge.

2 they / be in my team .
   _____
   _____

3 it / be an unusual job .
   _____
   _____

4 you / be his boss .
   _____
   _____

5 they / check customer service .
   _____
   _____

6 he / travel a lot .
   _____
   _____

7 she / work in the London office .
   _____
   _____

3 Make questions for these answers.

1 _Where's the trade fair?_
   The trade fair is in Frankfurt.
2 _____ ?
   The show ends on the May 20th.
3 _____ ?
   Yes, we're an international company.

4 _____ ?
   We manufacture rollercoasters.
5 _____ ?
   Yes, the company delivers products all over the world.
6 _____ ?
   No, I'm not in customer service.
7 _____ ?
   Yes, the site is large.

4 Fill in the gaps.

> install export supply manufacture
> deliver design advise

1 We usually _deliver_ orders the next day.
2 We _____ our products to China and Japan.
3 Our engineers _____ the equipment at the customer's factory.
4 We use computers to _____ our products.
5 They _____ the parts at their factory in France.
6 These two companies _____ us with spare parts for our machines.
7 We _____ new customers on the maintenance of the machines.

5 Fill in the chart.

> beef apple potato chicken roast
> haddock grilled lamb salmon fried
> broccoli cod salad mashed pea
> carrot leek strawberry

Meat	Fish	Vegetables	Fruit	Cooking or preparation
beef	haddock	potato	apple	roast

6 Match the pairs to make sentences.

1	We have	a	for the main course?
2	Are you ready to	b	for dessert, please?
3	I'd like soup	c	order now?
4	Could I have chicken	d	anything else to drink?
5	Could I have ice cream	e	we just have the bill, please?
6	Can I get you	f	for the starter.
7	No coffee, could	g	a reservation.

UNIT 2

1 Write the present continuous of the verbs.

1 They *'re building* the walls this morning. *(build)*

2 She _____ the project very well. *(not manage)*

3 What _____ the project manager _____ this morning? *(do)*

4 Where _____ the architect _____ today? *(work)*

5 The lights _____ at the moment. *(not work)*

6 We _____ problems with the budget. *(have)*

2 Fill in the gaps.

ahead of   behind   update   over
budget   complete   on schedule

1 Can you give me an _____*update*_____ ? Is the project _____ ?

2 They're opening early – they're _____ schedule.

3 We're spending too much. We're _____ budget.

4 They're running a month late. They're _____ schedule.

5 The costs are quite low. They're under _____ .

6 When can you _____ the decorating?

3 Fill in the gaps.

hard-working   reliable   adaptable   creative
confident   experienced   strong   analytical

1 She's very _____*experienced*_____ after 15 years in the job.

2 He's never behind schedule. He's so _____ .

3 She only takes a 20-minute break for lunch. She's really _____ .

4 They are a very _____ team. They always think of new ways of doing things.

5 He can work in lots of different situations, because he's so _____ .

6 He's very _____ and can quickly see what the problem is.

7 He sets clear objectives for his team. He's a very _____ leader.

8 She's a _____ speaker, even with people she doesn't know.

4 Write the gerund of the verbs.

1 He likes *solving* other people's problems. *(solve)*

2 The manager is only good at _____ our coffee break! *(organise)*

3 I enjoy _____ in very small teams. *(work)*

4 She's not very quick at _____ decisions. *(make)*

5 He's not good at _____ people. *(manage)*

6 He likes _____ on creative projects. *(work)*

5 Are these sentences sense (S) or nonsense (N)? Write S or N in the boxes.

1 I love scuba diving. It's a lot of fun. *S*

2 I can't stand boxing. I'd love to have a go at it. ☐

3 I can't play tennis, that's my problem. I'm good at it. ☐

4 I don't like watching football. It's not my cup of tea. ☐

5 I enjoy playing golf. I'm not interested in it. ☐

6 I'd love to have a go at underwater hockey. I bet it's good fun. ☐

UNIT 3

1 Match the pairs to make sentences. Write a–g in the boxes.

1 [b] There is a 20%
2 [ ] The delivery charge
3 [ ] You can save time and
4 [ ] All the products in that
5 [ ] People don't like
6 [ ] They deliver the goods
7 [ ] It's important to get

a money, if you shop online.
b discount on all products.
c directly from the warehouse.
d buying expensive goods online.
e is included in the price.
f a quote before you place an order.
g store are good quality.

2 Make comparisons. Use the correct form of the adjectives.

1 It's much _cheaper_ to book flights and hotels on the Internet. (+ cheap)
2 It's _____ _____ to buy a laptop in a store than online. (+ expensive)
3 Train travel in Europe is _____ _____ _____ flying nowadays. (= cheap)
4 It's a lot _____ and _____ to order goods directly from a warehouse. (+ good / + quick)
5 The service with the new manager is much _____ than with the old one. (+ bad)
6 It's _____ _____ to place an order with the new software. (– difficult)

3 Make superlatives. Use the correct form of the adjectives.

1 This is _the_ _most_ _advanced_ technology in the world. (+ advanced)
2 He has _____ _____ job in our company. (+ bad)
3 We guarantee that our products are

_____ _____ _____ .

(– expensive)
4 We have _____ _____ _____ offices in the city. (+ modern)
5 That's _____ _____ discount we can offer. (+ good)
6 This is _____ _____ room for meetings. (+ nice)

4 Match the pairs to make sentences. Write a–f in the boxes.

1 [f] The most important
2 [ ] The regulations make it
3 [ ] We have air-conditioning, so it's
4 [ ] There's only one possible
5 [ ] It's absolutely essential
6 [ ] It's quite a difficult

a not necessary to open the windows.
b to have good light to work in.
c compulsory to have fire exits.
d problem to solve.
e solution to this problem.
f thing is to finish the job on time.

5 Fill in the gaps.

island mountain ocean forest northern coast

1 We could see the southern _coast_ of England from the ferry.
2 Europe is in the _____ hemisphere.
3 The Pacific is the biggest _____ in the world.
4 That _____ is over 1,500 metres high.
5 Jersey is a small _____ near France.
6 The trees in the _____ were very high.

UNIT 4

1 Match the pairs. Write a–h in the boxes.

1 [d] This is simple.
2 [ ] My car doesn't use a lot of petrol.
3 [ ] This product is very safe.
4 [ ] The product was a flop.
5 [ ] This car never breaks down.
6 [ ] Lots of people buy this product.
7 [ ] This machine is quick and saves us time.

a It wasn't successful.
b It's very popular.
c It's very economical.
d It's not complicated.
e It's very efficient.
f It's very reliable.
g It isn't dangerous.

2 Fill in the gaps with *was*, *wasn't*, *were* or *weren't*.

1 A ___Was___ the advert a failure in Europe?

 B Yes, it _____ a complete flop.

2 A _____ the batteries very small?

 B No, they _____ quite big.

3 A _____ the vehicle very economical?

 B No. it _____ . The running costs _____ very high.

4 A _____ profits very low this quarter?

 B No, they _____ . Sales _____ very high.

3 Change the sentences. Use the adjectives and the word in brackets.

expensive   dangerous   low   fast   simple

1 That car is too slow. *(enough)*

 That car isn't fast enough.

2 This is not cheap enough. *(too)*

 _____

3 The price of this product is too high. *(enough)*

 _____

4 These products aren't safe enough. *(too)*

 _____

5 The design is too complicated. *(enough)*

 _____

4 **a** Make negative sentences.

1 He started his new job last week.

 He didn't start his new job last week.

2 They made the film in India.

 _____

3 They had a very big budget.

 _____

4 The project cost £2 million.

 _____

5 She finished the job on time.

 _____

6 They used very expensive computers.

 _____

b Make positive sentences.

1 The photos didn't look very good.

 The photos looked very good.

2 They didn't take a long time to finish the job.

 _____

3 They didn't want to use computers.

 _____

4 She didn't go to Malaysia.

 _____

5 I didn't drink coffee in the break.

 _____

6 They didn't eat lunch.

 _____

5 Fill in the gaps.

impossible   solve   work   trouble   solution

1 I couldn't ___solve___ the problem.

2 We had _____ with the new computer.

3 We used a special camera, but it still didn't _____ .

4 It was _____ to film at night.

5 I don't think there's an easy _____ to this problem.

6 Make questions for these answers.

1 When *did you buy it?*

 I bought it yesterday.

2 _____ ?

 No, she didn't work in the office today.

3 _____ ?

 Yes, he made a video.

4 Where _____ ?

 They saw the product in a supermarket.

5 _____ ?

 Yes, we found your office very easily.

6 When _____ ?

 I went there last week.

7 Fill in the gaps.

round   shopping   cooked   lie   cleaned   meal   gardening

1 The apartment was really dirty, so we *cleaned* it.

2 I was tired, so I had a _____ in.

3 We went out for a _____ .

4 I went _____ for a new computer.

5 It was warm and sunny, so we did some _____ .

6 She _____ a meal for six people.

7 We had friends _____ for dinner.

98

UNIT 5

1 Fill in the gaps.

> contact   speak   touch   give   look   back

1 I'll *speak* to the conference organiser about accommodation.
2 Will you _____ Max a call this afternoon?
3 I'll get in _____ with Jenny.
4 Can you _____ the supplier after the meeting?
5 Shall I get _____ to the sales manager?
6 I can't _____ into it now. I'm too busy.

2 Make offers and suggestions with *'ll* and *shall*.

1 I / do / it / later .
   I'll do it later.
2 we / them /call back ?
   _____
3 I / check / details / today .
   _____
4 I / her / give call / this afternoon .
   _____
5 I / contact / hotel ?
   _____
6 we / book / seats / now ?
   _____

3 Fill in the gaps.

> forward   discussed   find   following
> attached   confirm   hesitate

1 I'm writing to *confirm* my flight details.
2 Please _____ below the details of the hotel.
3 As _____ , we are arriving in Toronto at 14.45.
4 Please don't _____ to contact me, if you need further details.
5 I look _____ to meeting you again soon.
6 Please find _____ the schedule for the project.
7 _____ our phone conversation, I reserved your train tickets.

4 Present simple or present continuous? Fill in the gaps with the correct tense of the verb.

1 The flight *arrives* at 23.00. *(arrive)*
2 The conference _____ at 9.00 am. *(start)*
3 I _____ to a conference with my colleague. *(go)*
4 I _____ a presentation at the conference. *(give)*
5 The conference _____ on October 27th. *(finish)*
6 We _____ in San Francisco for four days. *(stay)*

5 Fill in the gaps.

> leaflet   guided   souvenirs
> peak   shuttle   map

1 The *map* of the city centre shows interesting places for tourists.
2 There is a _____ bus every hour from the airport to the hotel.
3 Most tourists buy _____ of their visit.
4 Many museums offer _____ tours.
5 This information _____ has a list of restaurants.
6 It's difficult to get theatre tickets during _____ periods.

UNIT 6

1 Make predictions using *will*.

1 I don't think / he / finish / on time .
   I don't think he'll finish on time.
2 personally, / I think / they / be / over budget .
   _____
3 I think / it / be / a flop .
   _____
4 the project / not / be / a success .
   _____
5 I don't think / we / solve / the problem .
   _____
6 the sales figures / not / improve / next month .
   _____

2 Write sentences with the same meaning. Use the words in brackets.

1 He's coming tomorrow. I'm certain about that. (definitely) *He's definitely coming tomorrow.*

2 It's likely they'll get the contract. (probably) _____

3 Maybe I'll go to Spain on holiday this year. (perhaps) _____

4 I'm sure there'll be a big a market for this product. (certainly) _____

5 Perhaps their profits will be better this quarter. (possibly) _____

3 Match the pairs of sentences. Write a–e in the boxes.

1 [c] She's planning to set lower targets.

2 [ ] She's hoping to finish the project early.

3 [ ] She's only 20 but her goal is to be chief executive.

4 [ ] She's aiming to increase sales very soon.

5 [ ] She's going to calculate the costs carefully.

a She's always optimistic about schedules.

b She has a good short-term marketing strategy.

c She wants people to meet their objectives more easily.

d She wants the budget to be realistic.

e She's very ambitious.

4 Make first conditional sentences with *if*.

1 flight be delayed / I stay at airport . *If the flight's delayed, I'll stay at the airport.*

2 suppliers not deliver it today / we not finish on time . _____

3 you work hard / you achieve your goal . _____

4 project not be successful / we lose a lot of money . _____

5 they not finish job / they work late tonight . _____

6 price not be too high / we increase sales . _____

5 Fill in the gaps.

allowance   discount   non-refundable   one-way   advance   excess   include

1 Can I get a _____discount_____ if I book early?

2 Does the price of the ticket _____ airport taxes?

3 You can't cancel the ticket – it's _____ .

4 The baggage _____ is 25 kilos.

5 There's an _____ baggage charge of £5 per kilo.

6 It's cheaper if you book in _____ .

7 Do you want a return ticket or just _____ ?

UNIT 7

1 Fill in the gaps.

Masters   joined   promoted   trainee   post   left   graduated

I studied French and Spanish at the University of London and [1] *graduated* in 2001. I accepted a [2] _____ at Flexco as a [3] _____ . Luckily Flexco paid for me to do a [4] _____ in Management. After two years I was [5] _____ to assistant manager of international sales, but I didn't like it. It was too stressful! I [6] _____ Flexco six months later and went to work for Practicon. I [7] _____ my current company, TZK, a few months ago and I'm very happy here.

2 Past simple or present perfect? Fill in the gaps with the correct tense of the verb.

1 I *'ve worked* on several big projects like this. (work)

2 I _____ with her on a project last year. (work)

3 I _____ a Masters in 1997. (do)

4 She _____ a lot of large teams, but this is the largest. (manage)

5 He _____ for six different companies during his career. (work)

6 I _____ this company in 2001. (join)

7 I _____ to nearly 40 different countries on business trips. (travel)

Grammar and vocabulary practice

3 Make sentences. Use the present perfect.

1 you / use / this programme before ?
Have you used this programme before?

2 I / not / see / this version before .
_____

3 you / work / with her before ?
_____

4 you / ever / visit / China ?
_____

5 I / never / visit / Canada .
_____

6 I / not / use / this system before .
_____

7 you / ever / live / in a different country ?
_____

4 Match the pairs to make sentences.
Write a–g in the boxes.

1 [g] They've made very good
2 [ ] Our engineers are two months
3 [ ] We're having trouble
4 [ ] This delay means that we're now
5 [ ] Our new sales executive
6 [ ] I've got some
7 [ ] I'm optimistic about the business

a installing the new machines.
b because things are going well.
c ahead of schedule.
d is doing well.
e two weeks behind schedule.
f good news – we've found a new supplier!
g progress in the last three weeks.

5 Fill in the gaps with *already*, *yet* or *so far*.

1 Have you finished ___*yet*___ ?

2 We have to build six units today, and we've only built two _____ .

3 I didn't plan to finish all the work today, but I've _____ done everything.

4 The work has gone well _____ , but we haven't done the hardest job _____ .

5 A Have you booked your flight _____ ?
   B No, I'm going to book it this afternoon.

6 A Can you send me the report?
   B I've _____ sent it to you. I emailed it yesterday.

6 Fill in the gaps.

> boring frightening happy hard
> interesting sad frightened relaxed
> bored incredible

1 It's ___*hard*___ to run a marathon, especially for the first time.

2 I'm _____ ! I want to go and do something fun!

3 The first time I went skiing I was a bit _____ .

4 I didn't win the race, but I was still _____ with third place.

5 The instructor was good. The lesson was very _____ .

6 We waited at the airport for hours. It was really _____ .

7 I lost one of my skis at high speed. It was really _____ .

8 I'm always _____ when I'm on holiday.

9 I went to India last year. It was _____ . I was so _____ to leave.

UNIT 8

1 Fill in the gaps.

> fell rose index currencies
> stock shares

1 We accept payment in all major ___*currencies*___ .

2 The FTSE index _____ 100 points yesterday to its lowest point in ten years.

3 The London _____ market is closed for the holidays.

4 We now hold 30% of the _____ in BM Products.

5 The CAC 40 is the stock market _____ in France.

6 The strong dollar _____ against the yen yesterday.

2 Make sentences. Use the present perfect.

1 what / happen / to share prices / today ?
What has happened to share prices today?

2 this month the FTSE / rise / 2% .
----

3 this year the price of oil / be / stable .
----

4 this week shares in Volkswagen / go down .
----

5 the Dow Jones index / fall / 5% so far today .
----

3 Match the pairs to make sentences. Look carefully at the tenses! Write a–f in the boxes.

1 [c] Last month property prices in the UK
2 [ ] This year house prices in Japan
3 [ ] So far this year house sales in
4 [ ] In the late 1980s house prices in
5 [ ] At the moment people
6 [ ] A two-bedroom flat in London

a are spending huge amounts of money on property.
b the UK started to rise.
c fell by 0.2%.
d the USA have stayed strong.
e have fallen.
f costs the same as a house in Liverpool.

4 Fill in the gaps.

| property   loan   mortgage   lend |
| unemployment   boom   interest   recession |

1 We took out a very big *mortgage* , when we bought our house.
2 I pay 18% _____ on my credit card.
3 The price of _____ is very high in London.
4 High levels of _____ are bad for the economy.
5 I need to get a _____ from the bank to buy a new car.
6 The bank won't _____ him any money.
7 The biggest _____ in the USA was in 1929, after the stock market crashed.
8 There is a _____ in the property market. Prices have never been so high.

5 Match the words to the definitions. Write a–g in the boxes.

1 [d] A person who introduces a television show.
2 [ ] A drama about everyday life, which you can watch every week on TV.
3 [ ] A person who takes part in a quiz or competition.
4 [ ] A foreign film which is in your language.
5 [ ] They interview famous people in this type of programme.
6 [ ] The written translation of the text of a foreign film.
7 [ ] A serious programme about nature, history, business or politics.

a subtitles   b contestant   c talk show
d presenter   e dubbed   f documentary
g soap opera

UNIT 9

1 Match the pairs to make sentences. Write a–g in the boxes.

1 [c] We have a new advertising
2 [ ] We promote our brand
3 [ ] We advertise on TV and in
4 [ ] Sometimes we market our
5 [ ] Our new logo is designed to
6 [ ] The football club found
7 [ ] Adverts in newspapers are

a a very effective way of marketing.
b brand in television commercials.
c strategy.
d in a very imaginative way.
e sponsorship for the under-18 team.
f business magazines.
g give us a more modern image.

2 Change the sentences from the active to the passive.

1 Millions of people saw the advert.
The advert was seen by millions of people.

2 A lot of businesspeople read this magazine every week.
----

3 Companies advertise lots of products on billboards.
----

4 They sponsored our basketball team.

----

5 This agency designed our new logo.

----

6 Our managing director signs all contracts.

----

3 Fill in the gaps.

> hire   invest   raise   go bankrupt   launch
> set up   cut costs   lay off

1 We ___*set up*___ the company five years ago.

2 The company couldn't _____ enough finance to expand.

3 Fortunately we found someone who wanted to _____ in our business.

4 We're planning to _____ our new product next year.

5 We _____ by closing one of our factories.

6 Business isn't good this year, so we are going to _____ some of our production team.

7 If our business doesn't improve rapidly we'll _____ .

8 It costs a lot of money to _____ experienced workers.

4 Fill in the gaps with adverbs.

1 She found a new job ___*easily*___ . *(easy)*

2 The new manager works _____ . *(hard)*

3 He plans everything very _____ . *(careful)*

4 Sales increased _____ last year. *(quick)*

5 We need to change our products _____ . *(significant)*

6 They're planning to _____ expand the business. *(gradual)*

5 Match the pairs. Write a–e in the boxes.

1 [d] Is it safe to pay by credit card?

2 [ ] Click here to join now.

3 [ ] I've bought some antivirus software.

4 [ ] It was easy to fill in the registration form online.

5 [ ] You need two pieces of information to log in.

a You have to have a user name and password.

b They didn't want much information.

c Members get full access to the site.

d Yes, this site has a secure server.

e It's important to install regular updates.

UNIT 10

1 Fill in the gaps.

> how   idea   could   why   about
> suggestions   not

1 That's a really interesting ___*idea*___ .

2 We _____ let people download direct from the Internet.

3 What _____ using different packaging?

4 Why _____ just change the shape of the box?

5 Any _____ about the marketing strategy?

6 _____ about using a new logo?

7 _____ don't we ask our customers what they want?

2 Complete the second conditional sentences. Use the correct forms of the verbs.

1 If CDs ___*didn't have*___ packaging, they ___*would be*___ cheaper. *(not have, be)*

2 Our CDs _____ more if they _____ cheaper. *(sell, be)*

3 If we _____ the price, we _____ more CDs. *(lower, sell)*

4 I think we _____ more CDs if we _____ them in bigger packs. *(sell, sell)*

5 If we _____ lateral thinking, we _____ better ideas. *(use, have)*

3 Fill in the gaps.

> have to   shouldn't   should
> don't have to   should

1 I don't think you ___*should*___ criticise other people's ideas. It's not helpful.

2 In my opinion we _____ change our logo because it's very well known by the public.

3 In our company you _____ agree with everything the boss says. She likes hearing different ideas.

4 You _____ always make it clear that you're criticising the idea, not the person.

5 You _____ use this safety equipment in the lab. It's a company rule.

4 Match the pairs to make sentences.
Write a–f in the boxes.

1 [b] I'm not sure
2 [ ] I'm worried about
3 [ ] I'm going to make a few proposals
4 [ ] I recommend that
5 [ ] We have to consider the
6 [ ] There are many benefits in cutting our

a unstable economic situation.
b about laying off staff at the moment.
c spending on advertising.
d we should build a new factory.
e expanding the business too quickly.
f for you to discuss.

5 Match the opposites. Write a–g in the boxes.

1 [d] The plane landed.
2 [ ] I missed my connection.
3 [ ] We were delayed.
4 [ ] I changed in London.
5 [ ] I rushed to the airport.
6 [ ] I cancelled my ticket.
7 [ ] They didn't give my money back.

a The flight was on time.
b I took a direct train.
c I took my time.
d We took off.
e I got a refund.
f I caught the train.
g I made a reservation.

UNIT 11

1 Fill in the gaps.

> over   under   out   around
> above   along   through   off

1 To get ___out___ of the building, go
   _____ the doors opposite reception.
2 Drive _____ this road for two kilometres –
   the station is on the right.
3 We drove all _____ the city yesterday but
   couldn't find the office.
4 Don't forget to get _____ the train in
   Birmingham.

5 The bridge goes _____ the A204 road
   near the town centre.
6 The Eurotunnel goes _____ the English
   channel.
7 A hovercraft flies just _____ the water.

2 Match the pairs to make sentences.

1 The motorway   a very light.
2 The train track   b about 1,000
                          kilograms.
3 The height of the   c is 1.2 metres
   bridge   wide.
4 The weight of this d is about 145
   car is   miles long.
5 This laptop weighs e is only 3.2
   only 1.2 kilos. It's   metres.

3 Fill in the gaps.

> regulations safety accidents procedure
> prevent health protective precautions

1 There are ___health___ and _____ signs in
   every part of the factory.
2 You must take safety _____ to avoid
   _____ .
3 The _____ say that you have to wear ear
   protection at all times.
4 Hard hats help to _____ injuries.
5 You must complete each_____ in the
   order on the list.
6 What _____ equipment do you need for
   this job?

4 Fill in the gaps with *must* or *mustn't*.

1 You ___must___ have a licence to drive a car.
2 You _____ smoke in the toilets on a
   plane.
3 You _____ drink lots of water when you
   run a marathon.
4 You _____ talk to a bus driver, when he's
   driving.
5 You _____ be over 14 to have a part-
   time job in the UK.
6 You _____ swim here. The lake is used
   for drinking water.
7 You _____ speak German and English to
   get a job as a Lufthansa pilot.
8 You _____ send dangerous items by
   mail.

5 Fill in the gaps.

> cabin balcony bunk adapters sauna
> nightclub baths shower dry laundry

1 Our _cabin_ on the cruise ship was quite small. There was only room for two _____ beds.
2 I tried the _____ last night but I found it far too hot.
3 The DJ in the _____ was really good fun.
4 The most expensive cabins had _____ but we only had a _____ .
5 The _____ cleaning service at the _____ was excellent.
6 You could buy international _____ for the electrical sockets.
7 We had an excellent view from the _____ outside our cabin.

UNIT 12

1 Match the pairs to make sentences. Write a–h in the boxes.

1 [f] Sally and Jenny, who are both away,
2 [ ] Jack has kindly agreed
3 [ ] The agenda
4 [ ] I think everyone has a copy
5 [ ] If you can't attend a meeting,
6 [ ] We didn't hold
7 [ ] We've called this meeting to
8 [ ] Let's discuss

a to chair the meeting today.
b of the minutes of the last meeting.
c a progress meeting last week. We were too busy.
d item four on the agenda.
e discuss the financial crisis.
f send their apologies.
g was circulated last week.
h send an email or phone to tell us.

2 Make sentences with time clauses.

1 we / email / you / when / get / home .
   We'll email you when we get home.
2 I / phone / hotel / as soon as / know / all the details .
   _____

3 the meeting / not start / until / the boss / be there .
   _____
4 she / be in contact / again / when / plane / land .
   _____
5 they / not leave / before / you / arrive .
   _____

3 Fill in the gaps.

> reluctant keen promised refused
> happy agreed

1 He said he wasn't _keen_ to have a formal meeting, but was _____ to talk over coffee.
2 I asked Jenny if we could change the date of the meeting and she _____ .
3 The travel agent _____ to give us a refund because we cancelled at the last minute.
4 I'm _____ to agree to this, because last time you didn't deliver on time.
5 He _____ to deliver the order on time.

4 Complete the reported speech sentences.

1 'I'll be late.'
   He said he _would be_ late.
2 'I'll circulate the minutes.'
   She promised she _____ the minutes.
3 'They can't attend the meeting.'
   They said they _____ the meeting.
4 'I have copy of the report.'
   I told him I _____ a copy of the report.
5 'I'll meet you later.'
   He said he _____ me later.
6 'We can deliver on time.'
   We told them we _____ on time.

5 Match the pairs. Write a–e in the boxes.

1 [d] How are you?
2 [ ] Sorry I'm late.
3 [ ] Do you mind if I make a call?
4 [ ] Shall we take a break?
5 [ ] Can I get you anything to drink?

a That's OK.
b No, I'm fine, thanks.
c Good idea.
d Fine, thank you.
e Not at all.

Grammar reference

1 GERUND

- We use a verb + *-ing* after verbs of like and dislike (*like/love/enjoy/ hate*, etc.).
  *He doesn't like **travelling**.*
- We also use the gerund after certain expressions which end with *at*.
  *I'm good at **thinking** of new ideas.*
- We can use the gerund as a noun.
  ***Managing** people isn't easy.*

2 ADJECTIVES

- Adjectives go before the noun they describe (or after the verb *be*).
  *It's a **new** computer.*
  *This computer is **new**.*
- Adjectives have only one form for singular and plural.
  *It's a **big** house with a **small** garden.*
  *They are **big** houses with **small** gardens.*

2.1 Comparatives

- We use the comparative to compare two things. The forms are:
  adjective + *-er* + *(than)*
  *This computer is **cheaper than** that one.*
  more/less + adjective + *(than)*
  *Shopping online is **less expensive than** shopping in a supermarket.*
  The form you use depends on the number of syllables in the adjective.
- For one-syllable adjectives ending in a consonant, add *-er*:
  *small > small**er**   cheap > cheap**er**
  fast > fast**er***
  (Some short adjectives double the final consonant: *big > bi**gg**er*)
- If a one-syllable adjective already ends in *-e*, you just add *-r*:
  *saf**e** > saf**er**   nic**e** > nic**er**   larg**e** > larg**er***
- If a two-syllable adjective ends in *-y*, take away the *-y* and add *-ier*:
  *bus**y** > bus**ier**   eas**y** > eas**ier***
- If a two-syllable adjective ends in a consonant, use *more* + adjective:
  *modern > **more** modern
  formal > **more** formal*

- With long adjectives of three or more syllables, use *more* + adjective:
  *expensive > **more** expensive
  economical > **more** economical*
  There is only one negative comparative form: *less* + adjective:
  ***less** cheap   **less** busy   **less** modern
  less expensive*
- There is no pattern to irregular adjectives. You have to learn the different forms of the comparative.
  *The results were **worse/better** than I expected.*
- We also use *(not) as ... as* to make comparisons.
  *We are **as busy** this month **as** we were last month. (= the same)*
  *The new system is **not as efficient as** the old one. (= less)*

2.2 Superlatives

- There are two different ways to make the positive superlative form of regular adjectives.
  The forms are:
  the + adjective + *-est*
  *China is **the biggest** market for our products.*
  the + *most/least* + adjective
  *It's **the least expensive** option.*
  The form you use depends on the number of syllables in the adjective.
- For one-syllable adjectives ending in a consonant, add *-est*:
  *small > the small**est**   cheap > the cheap**est**
  fast > the fast**est***
  (Some short adjectives double the final consonant: *big > bi**gg**est*)
- If a one-syllable adjective already ends in *-e*, you just add *-t*:
  *saf**e** > the saf**est**   nic**e** > the nic**est**
  larg**e** > the larg**est***
- If a two-syllable adjective ends in *-y*, take away the *-y* and add *-iest*:
  *bus**y** > the bus**iest**   eas**y** > the eas**iest***
- If a two-syllable adjective ends in a consonant, use *the most* + adjective:
  *modern > the **most** modern   formal > the **most** formal*

- With long adjectives of three or more syllables, use *the most* + adjective:

  *expensive > the **most** expensive   economical > the **most** economical*

- There is only one negative comparative form: *the least* + adjective:

  *the **least** cheap   the **least** busy
  the **least** modern   the **least** expensive*

- There is no pattern to irregular adjectives. You have to learn the different forms of the superlative.

  *These are the **best/worst** results since 1999.*

2.3 too/enough

- We use *too* to say 'more than necessary' or 'more than you need or want'. The form is:

  too + adjective

  *big > **too** big   small > **too** small*

- We also use *not … enough* to say 'not as much as you need or want'. The form is:

  not + adjective + *enough*

  *big > **not** big **enough**   small > **not** small **enough***

3   TALKING ABOUT THE PRESENT

3.1 Present simple

3.1.1 be

The verb *be* is irregular.

Positive

long form	short form
I am	I'm
you are	you're
he is	he's
she is	she's
it is	it's
we are	we're
they are	they're

Negatives

long form	short form
I am not	I'm not
you are not	you aren't / you're not
he is not	he isn't / he's not
she is not	she isn't / she's not
it is not	it isn't / it's not
we are not	we aren't / we're not
they are not	they aren't / they're not

Questions	Short answers	
	positive	negative
Am I … ?	Yes, I am.	No, I'm not. (one form)
Are you … ?	Yes, you are.	No, you aren't / you're not.
Is he … ?	Yes, he is.	No, he isn't / he's not.
Is she … ?	Yes, she is.	No, she isn't / she's not.
Is it … ?	Yes, it is.	No, it isn't / it's not.
Are we … ?	Yes, we are.	No, we aren't / we're not.
Are they … ?	Yes, they are.	No, they aren't / they're not.

- We use the short form in conversations. *Be* has two negative short forms. They are both common.

3.1.2 Other verbs

- We use the present simple to talk about routines, regular activities and things that are generally true.

  *Helen **works** in Manchester.*

  *She **goes** to work by train.*

- For company names we use the third person singular or the third person plural.

  *Vekoma **sell/sells** rollercoasters.*

Positive

I/you/we/they work

he/she/it work**s**

Negative

I/you/we/they **don't** work

he/she/it **doesn't** work

Questions	Short answers
Do I/you/we/they work?	Yes, I/you/we/they **do**. No, I/you/we/they **don't**.
Does he/she/it work?	Yes, he/she/it **does**. No, he/she/it **doesn't**.

(don't = do not, doesn't = does not)

- Normally, we use the short forms (*don't/doesn't*) in conversation.

- For most regular verbs, add an *-s* to the infinitive to make the third person singular.

  Add *-es* to *do*, *go*, and verbs ending in *-ch*, *-sh*, *-s* or *-x*. For verbs ending in consonant + *-y*, change *-y* to *-ies*.

Infinitive	he/she/it
live	live**s**
go	go**es**
do	do**es**
watch	watch**es**
fax	fax**es**
supply	suppl**ies**
study	stud**ies**

- We use *do* to make questions in the present simple, but *do* is also an ordinary verb:

  What do you **do**? – *I'm an accountant.*

  She **does** *aerobics at a sports club.*

3.2 Present continuous

- We use the present continuous to describe what's happening now.

  The form of the present continuous is:

  be + verb + *-ing*.

  Where's Nick? – He's **having** *lunch at the moment.*

  *They***'re visiting** *our new factory this week.*

  *I***'m working** *at home today.*

Positive

I'm	working
he's/she's/it's	going
you're/we're/they're	visiting

Negative

I'm not		working
he/she/it isn't	isn't / 's not	going
you/we/they aren't	aren't / 're not	visiting

Questions

Am I	working?
Is he/she/it	going?
Are you/we/they	visiting?

Short answers

positive

Yes, I am.

Yes, he/she it is.

Yes, you/we/they are.

negative

No, I'm not.

No, he/she/it	isn't / 's not.
No, you/we/they	aren't / 're not.

- If the infinitive of the verb ends in *-e*, remove the *-e* before adding *-ing*.

  *mak***e** › *mak***ing**

  *phon***e** › *phon***ing**

  *hav***e** › *hav***ing**

- With verbs that end with a consonant, vowel, consonant (for example: **swim**, **run**, **travel**) you double the last consonant.

run	ru**nn**ing
swim	swi**mm**ing
travel	trave**ll**ing

4 TALKING ABOUT THE PAST

4.1 Past simple

4.1.1 *be*

- The verb *be* is irregular. In the past simple we don't use *didn't* with *be*.

Positive

I/he/she/it was

you/we/they were

Negative

I/he/she/it wasn't

you/we/they weren't

Questions

Was I/he/she/it ...?

Were you/we/they ...?

Short answers

positive

Yes, I/he/she/it was.

Yes, you/we/they were.

negative

No, I/he/she/it wasn't.

No, you/we/they weren't.

- *Wasn't* and *weren't* are short forms for *was not* and *were not*. We normally use the short forms of the negative in conversation.

4.1.2 Regular verbs

- The form for the past simple is the same for all persons. Most regular verbs follow the same pattern.

  Positive: subject + infinitive + *-ed*

  He **talked** to Ben yesterday.

  Negative: subject + *didn't* + infinitive

  They **didn't discuss** the report.

  Question: *Did* + subject + infinitive

  Did you **talk** about the trip to China?

  Short answers: *Yes/No,* + subject + *did/didn't.*

  Yes, I did. / No, I didn't.

- For verbs ending in *-e*, just add *-d*, to make the positive form.

  phon**e**

  I phoned him, but he was in a meeting.

  receiv**e**

  We received your order last Monday.

- For verbs ending in consonant + *-y*, change *-y* to *-ied.*

  supp**ly**

  Last year we supplied all their stores.

  stu**dy**

  She stud**ied** German for two years.

4.1.3 Irregular verbs

See the irregular verb list on page 113.

4.2 Present perfect

4.2.1 Regular verbs

- The form of the present perfect is:

  have/has + the past participle

  The past participle of regular verbs is: infinitive + *-ed*

  work › work**ed**

  live › liv**ed**

  start › start**ed**

  Positive: subject + *have/has* + past participle

  *I've **finished** the report.*

  Negative: subject + *haven't/hasn't* + past participle

  He **hasn't arrived** at the airport yet.

  Questions: *Have/Has* + past participle

  Have you **phoned** Tony today?

  Short answers: *Yes/No,* + subject + *have/haven't*

  Yes, I have. / No, I haven't.

4.2.2 Irregular verbs

See the irregular verb list on page 113.

4.2.3 Present perfect: past experience

- We use the present perfect to talk about general experience in the past.

  *She's **worked** in Switzerland, France and Italy.*

  *He **hasn't been** to Asia.*

  *I've never **had** a job with an advertising agency.*

  Have you **used** this software?

- If you talk about specific moments and events in the past, after a *Have you ever ...?* question, use the past simple, not the present perfect.

  Have you ever worked for a finance company? – Yes, I **worked** for Citicorp in 1996.

  Have you ever studied business management? – Yes, I **did** an MBA at Harvard.

4.2.4 Present perfect with *yet, already, so far*

- *Yet* = 'before now'. We use *yet* with the present perfect with questions and negatives (but not in positive sentences).

  *Have you sent the email **yet**?*

  *They haven't made a decision **yet**.*

- *Already* = 'at a time in the past'.

  *We've **already** designed the machine.*

- *So far* = 'until now'

  *I've checked half of the order **so far**.*

4.2.5 Present perfect with *today, this week/ month/year*

- We use the present perfect with these time expressions to describe actions that are not finished at the time of speaking.

  *Share prices in BP **have risen** 1% **this morning**. (It is not yet 12.00.)*

  *The price of steel **has gone up this week**. (It is not yet the end of the week.)*

  *The Dow Jones index **has fallen** 8% **this year**. (It is not yet the end of the year.)*

5 TALKING ABOUT THE FUTURE

5.1 Present continuous: future arrangements

- We use the present continuous to talk about definite arrangements for the future.

  *She's **presenting** the new product on Friday.*

  *I'm **going** to Milan next week.*

5.2 Present simple tense for future timetables.

- We use the present simple to talk about future timetables and schedules (often with specific times or dates).

  *I **arrive** at 12.00.*

  *The conference **starts** on Monday 17th April.*

5.3 Future with *going to*

- We use *going to* to talk about plans and intentions.

  The form is: *be + going to + infinitive.*

- Positive:

  *We**'re going to** discuss the plans with the team.*

- Negative:

  *They **aren't** / They**'re not going to** have a meeting today.*

- Questions and short answers:

  ***Is** she **going to** talk about the new project? – Yes, she **is**. / No, she **isn't**.*

5.4 Future with *will*

5.4.1 Predictions with *will*

- We use *will* to predict what will happen in the future. It is often used with expressions of opinion (*I think/I'm sure*) or with words such as *certainly, maybe, probably, definitely, possibly, perhaps.*

  *I **think** the plan **will** work.*

  *I **don't think** she'll get here on time. (she'll = she will)*

  *It'll definitely be a flop. Yes, I'm sure it **won't** work. (won't = will not)*

- When speaking, *will* is nearly always shortened to *'ll* after pronouns and very often after nouns but the short form after nouns is never written.

  We can say: 'I think the **plan'll** work.'

  We always write: I think the **plan will** work. (NOT ~~I think the plan'll work~~.)

5.4.2 Time expressions with *will*

- We use expressions such as *when, as soon as, before* and *until* to make it clear when we are going to do something. For the first clause in the sentence we use *will* + infinitive, but after the time expression (for the second clause) we use a present tense.

  *I**'ll** contact you **when** I **get** home.*

  *We**'ll** prepare the plan **before** the meeting **starts**.*

  *We**'ll** be very busy **until** the project **is finished**.*

*I**'ll** email you **as soon as** I **reach** the office. (NOT ~~I'll email you as soon as I'll reach the office~~.)*

CONDITIONAL

6.1 First conditional

- The form of the first conditional is:

  If + present simple + will

  ***If** I see Jim, I**'ll** ask him for a copy of the agenda. (I'll = I will)*

- We use first conditional for things which will possibly happen.

  ***If** the plan **works** we'll start the project tomorrow.*

  ***If** demand grows, we**'ll** increase production.*

  Sometimes *if* comes in the middle of the sentence. The form of the first conditional is then:

  will + if + present simple.

  *It**'ll** be impossible to achieve our objectives, **if** we**'re** behind schedule.*

6.2 Second conditional

- The form of the second conditional is:

  If + past simple + would

  ***If** I **went** to the conference, I**'d** fly back the next day. (I'd = I would)*

- We use the second conditional when we imagine what might happen in the future.

  ***If** we **travelled** by car, we**'d** get there quicker.*

  ***If** you **worked** harder, you**'d** be more successful.*

  Sometimes *if* comes in the middle of the sentence. The form of the second conditional is then:

  would + if + past simple

  *It **would** be lighter **if** we **used** plastic.*

7

PASSIVE

- The passive is less direct than the active. It is often used to describe processes. We frequently use the passive when it's not important to know what or who did the action.

  The form of the passive is:

  be + past participle

  Active: *Lots of people read The Times.*

  Passive: *The Times **is read** by lots of people.*

Active: *They showed the adverts on TV last month*.

Passive: *The adverts **were shown** on TV last month*.

(For the past participles of irregular verbs see the verb list on page 113.)

8 OFFERS AND SUGGESTIONS

8.1 *shall*

- We use *shall* and *let's* to make suggestions.
  The forms are:
  Shall + I/we + infinitive?
  Let's + infinitive
- Use *Shall I ...?* when you offer to do something or suggest doing something.
  ***Shall I** do the photocopies for you?*
  ***Shall I** book the flights?*
- Use *Shall we ...?* when you want to suggest doing something with someone else.
  ***Shall we** meet next week?*
  ***Shall we** talk about the design?*

8.2 *will*: spontaneous decisions and offers

- We use *will* when we offer or quickly decide to do something at the time of speaking:
  *Can I give you the number? – Yes, **I'll** write it down.*
  *Antonio's having lunch. – OK, **I'll** call back later.*
  *The photocopier isn't working. – Right, **I'll** call someone to fix it.*
  (NOT ~~I call someone ...~~)
- The short form of *will* is *'ll*. Always use the short form when you speak, for offers and decisions.

9 MODAL VERBS

9.1 *should*

- We use *should* when we want to say that it's a good/bad idea to do something.
  The form is:
  positive and negative: subject + *should/shouldn't* + infinitive
  *I think we **should** sell this at a lower price.*
  *In my view, we **shouldn't** build the new factory there.*
  questions: *Should + subject + infinitive?*
  ***Should** we stay here? What do you think?*

9.2 *have to*

- We use *have to* when it's necessary to do something and *don't have to* when you don't need to do something.
  The form is:
  positive: subject + *have/has to* + infinitive
  *You **have to** wear a hard hat in the building.*
  negative: subject + *don't/doesn't have to* + infinitive
  *You **don't have to** wear protective clothing here. It's quite safe.*
  questions: *Do/Does + subject + have to + infinitive?*
  ***Do** I **have to** wear protective clothes?*

9.3 *must*

- We also use *must* instead of *have/has to* to say 'it's necessary to do something'. It has the same meaning as *have to*, but is used less often.
  The form is:
  positive: subject + *must* + infinitive
  *You **must** be over 17 to drive a car UK.*
- *Mustn't* has a completely different meaning from *don't have to*. It means that something is 'not allowed or permitted'.
  negative: subject + *mustn't* + infinitive
  *You **mustn't** smoke in the lift.*

10 ADVERBS OF MANNER

- Adverbs of manner describe actions in more detail. They normally come at the end of a sentence.
  *She drives **carefully**.*
  *He drove **fast**.*
  *They work **well**.*
- The form of most adverbs is: adjectives + *-ly*
  *quick › quick**ly***
  *serious › serious**ly***
  *quiet › quiet**ly***
- Some adverbs have the same form as the adjective:
  *hard › **hard**   fast › **fast**   friendly › **friendly***
- A few adverbs are irregular:
  *good › **well***

11 PREPOSITIONS

11.1 Location/Position

- These prepositions describe where a place, person or thing is.

  Madrid is **in** Spain, in the centre.

  Canton is **near** Hong Kong.

  His office is **above** the shop.

  The submarine is **under** the sea.

  The computer is **on** the desk.

  He's **at** the station now.

  She's **at** home today.

11.2 Movement

- These prepositions describe the direction and movement of something or someone.

  You can go **into** the city centre from the airport by taxi.

  The best way **out of** the terminal is through these doors.

  You have to get **off** the bus here.

  The bridge goes **across** the river.

  I walked **around** the office but I couldn't find you.

  The Eurotunnel goes **under** the English Channel.

  These stairs only go **up** to the fourth floor.

  He drove **along** the street.

12 REPORTED SPEECH

- We use reported speech when we describe what somebody said.

- When the verb in direct speech is *will* or *can* the form is:

  past simple + subject + *would/could*

  Direct speech: '*I'll be late.*'

  Reported speech: He **told** me he **would** be late.

  Direct speech: '*We can't deliver on time.*'

  Reported speech: They **said** they **couldn't** deliver on time.

- For all other verbs the form is:

  past simple + subject + past simple

  Direct speech: '*The work is on schedule.*'

  Reported speech: She **told** me the work **was** on schedule.

- There are other reporting verbs we can use to describe what somebody said (*promise, offer, refuse, agree,* etc.).

  He **agreed** to give a presentation.

  I **promised** to be there on time.

IRREGULAR VERBS

Infinitive	Past simple	Past participle
be	was/were	been
become	became	become
begin	began	begun
break	broke	broken
bring	brought	brought
build	built	built
buy	bought	bought
catch	caught	caught
choose	chose	chosen
come	came	come
cost	cost	cost
cut	cut	cut
do	did	done
draw	drew	drawn
drink	drank	drunk
drive	drove	driven
eat	ate	eaten
fall	fell	fallen
feel	felt	felt
find	found	found
fly	flew	flown
forget	forgot	forgotten
get	got	got
give	gave	given
go	went	gone
have	had	had
hear	heard /hɜːd/	heard
keep	kept	kept
know	knew	known
learn	learned/learnt	learned/learnt
leave	left	left
lose	lost	lost
make	made	made
meet	met	met
pay	paid	paid
put	put	put
read	read /red/	read
ring	rang	rung
run	ran	run

say	said	said
see	saw	seen
sell	sold	sold
send	sent	sent
sing	sang	sung
sleep	slept	slept
speak	spoke	spoken
spend	spent	spent
stand	stood	stood
swim	swam	swum
take	took	taken
teach	taught	taught
tell	told	told
think	thought	thought
throw	threw	thrown
understand	understood	understood
wake	woke	woken
wear	wore	worn
win	won	won
write	wrote	written

Transcripts

▶▶ 1

OK. Welcome everybody. Ah, my name's Ivan Magnusson. I'm your trainer for this two-day course. A course, as you know, called International Customer Service. Um ... to begin, I just want to explain, quickly, what I do. And then you can talk about your jobs. So I'm an export consultant. I specialise in services ...

▶▶ 2

Ella	My name's Ella Grady. I'm in the customer service department. I'm the European customer service manager. So, um ... I look after customer service for Europe.
Ivan	So are you in charge of the department?
Ella	I'm not the department manager, no. I report to the customer service manager. *He's* in charge of the department.
David	She reports to me!
Ivan	Ah! The boss is here!
David	I'm afraid so!
Ivan	And is your boss here?
David	No, she isn't on the course. Fortunately!
Ivan	I see. So, Ella, you aren't the department manager, but do you have a team ... in the department?
Ella	Yeah, I manage a small team of assistants. Five people. They're not all here – just two of them.
Ivan	Right. And how big is the region you look after?
Ella	We're responsible for customers in Europe, um ... eighteen countries, altogether.
Ivan	And do you have direct contact with customers? Do you speak to them?
Ella	Oh yes. The difficult ones, usually! I deal with problems most of the time.
Ivan	So you deal with difficult customers?
Ella	Quite a lot, yes.
David	She has a difficult boss, as well!
Ivan	Oh, I see!

▶▶ 4

Ivan	OK. Next, I want to give you some examples of bad customer service in hotels. Why hotels? Well, I have a secret job – a part-time job. I'm a spy. ... I know I don't look like James Bond, but it's perfectly true. I work for a hotel company. It's a chain of hotels. There are about ten other people who do this job – I'm not the only one. And ... we check customer service in the hotels we stay in. When I travel on business, I stay in a hotel that's in the chain. So ... as a spy, I check the quality of service. And after my stay, I write a report, um ... it doesn't take long. And, in return, my room's free. I don't pay.
David	So, people who do this, people like you, do it part-time? They travel a lot?
Ivan	That's right. Obviously, you have to stay in hotels

a lot. For me, it's good, because I travel with my job as a trainer. And, also, I'm in customer service, so ...

David	You're the perfect secret agent.
Ivan	Yeah. And I enjoy it. I don't like the paperwork, but the rest is good fun ... OK, let's look at some examples of bad customer service ...

▶▶ 6

(Rep = Representative)

Woman	So you make plastic animals.
Rep	That's right. All life-size. Cows, horses, sheep ...
Woman	They're very realistic. ... Oh, and they move!
Rep	Their heads move. They make sounds, if you just touch them ...
Woman	Oh!
Rep	They don't walk! Our customers prefer them to stay in one place.
Woman	Yes, right. So who are your customers? Where do you sell these things?
Rep	We sell a lot to fun parks, shopping centres, playgrounds ... Children all over the world love them. We export to twenty-five countries.
Woman	Really? I manage a small fun park in Germany. It's for children up to twelve years old.
Rep	Well, these are perfect for that age. We have a lot of customers in Germany. We work with a company called DDA, in Frankfurt. They install our products, and look after maintenance and after-sales service for all our German customers.
Woman	Right. So what country are you from?
Rep	From Canada. We have a factory near Montreal. We manufacture all our products there.
Woman	Oh, I see. ... Can I just ...?
Rep	Sure ...

▶▶ 8

1

Waiter	Everything OK?
David	Yes, fine thanks. Excellent.
Waiter	Can I get you anything else to drink? Or to eat?
David	Nothing for me. I'm fine, thanks. Ivan?
Ivan	No thanks. I'm full, thank you.
David	I think we're all OK. I think it's time to get back, actually. Could we have the bill, please?
Waiter	Sure.

2

Waiter	Hello.
Ivan	Hello. We have a reservation. The name's Magnusson. A table for three.
Waiter	Yes, OK. If you'd like to come this way, please.
Ivan	Thanks.

3

Waiter	Dessert?
Ella	Yes, could I have the apple pie, please.
Waiter	Apple pie.
David	Just a coffee for me, please. … Would anyone else like coffee?
Ella	I'll have one after my dessert.
Waiter	OK. Would anyone else like dessert?

4

Waiter	Are you ready to order?
Ella	Yes. For me, um … To start, the tomato soup, please.
David	Yes, the same for me, please. The tomato soup.
Waiter	What would you like for the main course?
Ella	I'd like salmon with rice and peas, please.
David	The lamb, with peas and carrots for me, please. Ivan?
Ivan	I don't want a starter, just a main course. Can I have steak, chips and peas, please?
Waiter	How would you like the steak?
Ivan	Um … Medium, please.

▶▶ 9

Vanessa	So where are you working, exactly, in France?
John	In the Jura. It's not far from Switzerland.
Vanessa	Right. And you're building a hotel?
John	We're converting a farmhouse into a hotel. It's very, um … it's a very old house. When we started, it had no windows, no doors … it was a ruin, basically.
Vanessa	And now?
John	Well, now, most of the work's complete. I'm staying in one of the rooms, in fact. So, um, I'm the first guest.
Vanessa	You're the boss, though, so you're not paying.
John	Oh, I'm paying! This project's costing a fortune!
Vanessa	I see. Well, that's one of my questions, actually. What's your budget?
John	Um … the total budget's five hundred and sixty thousand euros … and I'm paying half of that. Richard and Kathy Mills are paying the rest. They're my business partners.
Vanessa	And your business partners are hotel managers. Is that right?
John	That's right. I'm managing the project – the construction. And they're still living and working in the UK at the moment, organising the website and the marketing material, you know, brochures and things. Then they plan to live here and manage the hotel when it's finished.
Vanessa	I see. So, how long are you staying in France? What's the schedule, from start to finish?
John	Um … eighteen months. And we're more or less on schedule. At the moment, we're working on the bathrooms. We're having one or two problems with …

▶▶ 11

Rowan	So, the main thing is, we want creative people.
Judith	Mmm, yes, and creative people who can work hard. We're looking for young people, it's probably their first job, they've got no experience, um … so I think we need to make that clear. It's hard work. And even little things – getting to work on time in the morning, for example … the simple things are extremely important. We want reliable people. It sounds obvious, but …
Rowan	Yeah. We want people who are professional. That's …
Judith	Yes, that's the word.
Rowan	What … extra skills does a creative person need to be a professional? I mean, for example, we want them to work with *different* people as well – to change teams. That's one of our creative strategies, isn't it? We don't have the same people working together all the time.
Judith	Yes. So they need to cope with change.
Rowan	To cope with stress.
Judith	Sure.
Rowan	They need the confidence to present and explain ideas.
Judith	That's true.
Rowan	And there's the problem of understanding what the clients want. It's not always clear.
Judith	That's the manager's job, though. The creative team aren't responsible for analysing the client's needs. Later on, when we talk about …

▶▶ 13

Judith	Marco works for PAF, he's in the creative department, we know him, he knows us … but is that an advantage?
Rowan	Well, we want someone to manage the department. We need a manager to make the new strategy work. We don't really need new ideas. Marco's experienced, he knows the company well, and he knows what we want. I think his experience with PAF is a big advantage. Hiring someone new is … it's obviously a risk.
Judith	Yeah. But making Marco the department manager's also a risk. OK, he enjoys working for the company, he's not going to leave suddenly, he's popular in the department, but … that doesn't mean he's good at managing a team.
Rowan	But the number one priority is the new strategy. The manager has to sell the new strategy to the team. We know Marco's a good salesman. He likes selling ideas.
Judith	Yeah. … But, what about the other people in the department? They work *with* him at the moment. What happens if they have to work *for* him?
Rowan	Oh, I think he can cope with all that …

Woman	So, are you watching the cup final this weekend?
Man	Um … no, I don't think so.
Woman	Don't you like football?
Man	No. I can't stand it. Sorry to sound so miserable!
Woman	Mmm, I hate it too, but I watch the World Cup Final.
Man	I can't play, that's my problem. I'm hopeless at it! If I'm not very good at a sport, I don't like watching it.
Woman	So what do you like, then?
Man	I play golf.
Woman	Oh right. … My husband plays. I'm not interested in it, though. It's … not my cup of tea. He plays golf, I go horse riding.
Man	Oh, right. Well you could play polo – both of you. That's half horse riding, half golf! … I'd love to have a go at riding, actually. I bet it's good fun.
Woman	Oh, it's great fun.
Man	So, do you have your own horse?
Woman	No. I'd love to have one, but, um … it's expensive.
Man	Yeah. I'm quite interested in tropical fish. I'd like to have an aquarium, but … it's a problem if you travel a lot …
Woman	Tropical fish?
Man	Yeah. I'd like to have some piranhas.
Woman	Piranhas?
Man	Well, they say a hundred piranhas can eat a horse in less than five minutes!
Woman	Oh!
Man	I'm not sure if that includes the rider or not …

Lionel	Marilyn, these are both top quality products! The quality's the same.
Marilyn	I know. But they don't look the same. The one from Gild looks like a modern vacuum cleaner. This Aero …
Lionel	Aerosaurus.
Marilyn	Yeah. It looks like something from the 1960s.
Lionel	Well of course it does. It's a retro look.
Marilyn	I know, but what do most customers want? Do they want to pay a reasonable price for a modern vacuum cleaner, or pay more for something that looks forty years old?
Lionel	Yes, but surely we don't want just another 'modern' vacuum cleaner, that's the same as all the other products we sell? We need something different. OK, the Aerosaurus is more expensive. But it's *different* … And Suntra is making a good offer. Look – twelve percent discount – Gild is only offering five percent. Suntra is offering cheaper delivery, as well. We can make a bigger profit margin.
Marilyn	We can make a bigger margin, but we can only make a good profit if we sell enough vacuum cleaners. How many of these Aero…sauruses can we sell? I mean, look at it. It looks like a dinosaur!
Lionel	Of course it does! That's why people will love it! Just listen to it!

Interviewer	So, when you design an office, where do you start?
Steve	Well, the first question is, how much space do you need? And that's one of the most difficult questions, sometimes, because for most people, it's difficult to say, oh I need … fifteen square metres, for example. So you have to look at what people need to do in the office, look at what equipment they need – you know, most people need a phone, a computer, um … a desk! Then there's shared equipment, … you normally have a room with a photocopier, printers … a fax machine, possibly.
Interviewer	A coffee machine.
Steve	Oh, a coffee machine is essential! It's important where you put it. Do you put it in a corridor, with no windows … or next to the toilets … you know, so people have short coffee breaks. Or do you have a nice coffee area, with seats … big windows …? Daylight – that's a big consideration. Light's extremely important.
Interviewer	So you want big windows, if possible.
Steve	Yeah, you usually want a lot of light.
Interviewer	What do you think of open-plan offices? Do you like that sort of design?
Steve	Well, an open-plan office isn't really a design, is it? It's just a big room, um … But we're talking about the requirements for offices, and the most important question is money. You know, cost is always the biggest problem. At the end of the day, walls cost money. If they're not an essential requirement, then why have them? With anything that costs money, clients always ask, is it really necessary? Offices are expensive, even if you only have what's in the regulations – what's compulsory. So, if something's an optional extra …

Caroline	So, what do you think of Hawaii?
Alistair	Fantastic. The beaches are amazing. We've got some good surfing beaches in New Zealand, but here it's … well, the weather's a lot warmer, that's the first difference … at this time of year, anyway.
Caroline	Of course, it's winter in New Zealand, isn't it?
Alistair	Yeah. It'll soon be spring, though.
Caroline	I'd like to go, actually … maybe not this year, but … possibly next year.
Alistair	To New Zealand?
Caroline	Yeah. What's the best time of year to visit?
Alistair	Early summer's nice. Late December, early January.
Caroline	And what's the weather like?
Alistair	Pretty hot, usually. You can have Christmas dinner on the beach, no problem! But there's a lot more to do than just sit on a beach, obviously.

Caroline	Oh, sure. So, what are the best places to see?
Alistair	The nicest part of the country's the South Island, in my opinion, anyway. You go to the mountains there, the Southern Alps, and it's ... oh, it's beautiful.
Caroline	So, do you need a car, to travel round?
Alistair	Yeah. Or you can rent a camper van. That's what a lot of people do. There are hundreds of campsites, where you can ... you know ... park and ...
Caroline	Yeah. Yeah.
Alistair	I know that area pretty well, so ...
Caroline	So, can you recommend some campsites?
Alistair	Yeah, I can give you some good addresses. There's one campsite, next to a lake ...

▶▶ 24

Rob	So, to start with, I want to talk about ... the bicycle – a very successful invention. Any ideas why? What are the main advantages of bikes?
Woman 1	They don't cost much.
Rob	OK.
Man	They're not complicated.
Rob	They're easy to use, yeah.
Woman 1	Not too easy when you're going uphill!
Rob	No, that's true. Let's say 'simple'.
Woman 2	Running costs are low.
Rob	OK, yeah. Very cheap to run.
Man	They don't often break down.
Rob	Yeah. Reliable.
Woman 1	They're safe. Well ...
Rob	They're not too dangerous. OK. ... So, a successful invention, for all those reasons. And, with modern bikes, we have a good example of using the latest materials for a design that's over a hundred years old.

▶▶ 25

So, to sum up, then. Why are bicycles popular? They're cheap, simple, economical and efficient, reliable and safe. Now, that checklist is the same, no matter what sort of ...

▶▶ 26

There were lots of problems with the Sinclair C5. The biggest problem, I think, was ... it was too small, and especially, too low. Because it was so low, it was difficult for other drivers to see you. It was actually quite dangerous. And, obviously, if you're very low, and it's raining, then there's water splashing on you from cars. And then there was the battery. It was heavy. It wasn't very powerful, every night you had to recharge it. I mean ... forget it!

▶▶ 27

Jake	So this is quite an easy project ... certainly compared with the one we did last month, at a chemicals factory. It was, um ... quite a challenge!
Client	At a chemicals factory?
Jake	Yeah. It was a marketing video, for a chemicals company. They wanted to film different ... parts of the factory. The first problem was the heat. It was, ... I don't know what the temperature was, exactly, but it was *extremely* hot.
Client	So it was difficult to work?
Jake	Well, the trouble was, it was too hot for the camera.
Client	Oh, right. So what did you do?
Jake	We put the camera in a box, to protect it. We made a box, with a small hole in the front ...
Client	Yeah.
Jake	And, we filmed with the camera in the box.
Client	And did it work?
Jake	Yeah, it worked OK.
Client	So how did you make the box? What did you use?
Jake	Just wood. Nothing complicated. ... So, anyway, we finished filming in this hot area ... and then they wanted us to film with no light. They had another production process where, um ... they couldn't have any light at all. It was completely black.
Client	And they wanted you to film it?
Jake	Yeah.
Client	So what did you say?
Jake	I said, no, it's impossible. They thought maybe we could use a special camera or something, but, um ... it wasn't possible. ... So, filming in your offices isn't a big problem!
Client	Well, after that, no! So, when can you start setting up ...

▶▶ 28

Tessa	So, did you have a good weekend, Dave?
Dave	Yeah, OK, thanks. It was nice to have some warm weather for a change. We ate outside yesterday, at lunchtime. We sat outside in the garden.
Tessa	Did you?
Dave	Yeah. We wanted to have a barbecue, actually, but I forgot to buy some charcoal, so ...
Tessa	Oh, no. You didn't have people coming round?
Dave	Oh, no. It was just me and my wife, so ... it wasn't too bad. In fact, I was quite pleased. Normally, when we have a barbecue, I do the cooking, you see. But otherwise my wife cooks, so ...
Tessa	So you slept in the sun, and your wife did all the cooking!
Dave	Well ... I wasn't asleep – I had one eye open ... so I could see when it was ready! No, actually, I had quite a busy weekend. I put a new front door on the house on Saturday. It was a bigger job than I thought, actually. I got up early on Saturday and worked all day. Then on Sunday, I got up early and painted it ... What about you? What did you do?
Tessa	Not much really. Um, we went to the cinema on Saturday night.
Dave	Oh yeah? What did you see?
Tessa	Oh, it wasn't very good. It was that new film with ...

Michael Hello.

Sylvie Hello. Is that Michael?

Michael Speaking.

Sylvie Hi Michael, it's Sylvie in Brussels.

Michael Hi Sylvie, how are you?

Sylvie Fine, thanks. You?

Michael Yeah, very well, thanks.

Sylvie Are you getting ready for the conference next month?

Michael Um ... not really. What about you?

Sylvie Well, that's what I'm phoning about, actually. How are you going to San Francisco? Are you flying direct from Dublin?

Michael Um ... well, I still need to book my flight. But I'll probably have to change in ... either in London or ... in Amsterdam. What about you?

Sylvie Well, I still need to book my flight, from Amsterdam. So, um ...

Michael Well, shall we catch the same flight?

Sylvie Yeah. That's what I thought, actually. Then we can work on the plane.

Michael Yeah, that makes sense. So I need to book a flight to Amsterdam, then. Shall I look into flights to San Francisco, as well?

Sylvie Um ... yeah, if that's OK.

Michael Yeah, no problem. I'll look on the Internet after lunch and, um ... I'll call you back. What about booking a hotel?

Sylvie Um ... Well, shall I contact the San Francisco office ... see if they know any good places? I can get in touch with Rita.

Michael Yeah, good idea.

Sylvie I'll give her a call this afternoon, as soon as the office opens.

Michael Excellent. So I'll look into flights. And, um ... I'll get back to you.

Sylvie Great. Shall we speak at about four thirty?

Michael Yes, fine. I'll call you then.

Sylvie OK. Bye.

Michael Thanks for calling, Sylvie. Bye.

▶▶ 31

1 Yes, I'll call him.
2 I talked to Christine, and there's no problem.
3 I email the minutes to everyone.
4 Yes, I'll contact him.

▶▶ 32

Naomi So, when's the best time to meet, for you? I'm free next week.

Tom Um ... I can't make it next week. I'm ... I'm busy all week. The week after's OK for me.

Naomi The week after. What about Monday? Monday, December the twelfth?

Tom Yes, that's OK for me.

Naomi In the morning?

Tom Yeah.

Naomi Half past nine?

Tom Nine thirty? Yeah, that's fine.

Naomi OK. Monday, December the twelfth at nine thirty, then.

Tom And can you send me an agenda?

Naomi Yes, I'll write an agenda this morning, and send it to you this afternoon.

Tom Excellent. OK, so I look forward to receiving that, and I'll see you on the twelfth.

Naomi OK. I look forward to seeing you then.

Tom OK. Bye.

Naomi Bye.

▶▶ 34

1 **A** Hi.
  B Hello. Do you have any information about Alcatraz? Any ... booklets or (*beep*)?
  A Yes. Just behind you, on the shelf, there.
  B Ah, OK. Thank you.

2 **A** Hi.
  B Hi. Is there anywhere near here where you can buy gifts ... and (*beep*)?
  A Yeah. If you turn right out of the door, then take the first right, there are gift shops all along the ... the street, there.
  B OK. Thanks very much.

3 **B** Can you visit the museum all day? What are the opening times?
  A It opens at ten and closes at five. If you want to take a (*beep*), they start every hour, on the hour and last ... I think they last forty-five minutes, but I'll just check ...

4 **B** Excuse me. Have you got any street (*beep*)?
  A Sure.
  B ... Thanks. How much are they?
  A They're free.

▶▶ 36

Interviewer What do you think about the location of the resort, near Berlin?

Caroline Well, the reason it's there is, simply, because there was already a dome there. Tropical Islands Resort didn't build the dome. They bought it, for quite a low price. A company called CargoLifter built the dome as a factory, to make big airships. But CargoLifter went out of business and had to sell the dome. So Tropical Islands bought it and ... so they had very low construction costs.

Interviewer So, do you think the resort'll be successful in the long term?

Caroline Possibly. I think it'll probably be quite popular in the short term ... in the first few months. I think a lot of people'll probably come to have a look ... they'll want to see what it's like. After that, it depends what they think of it.

Interviewer Some people say this resort won't help to make forecasts for other resorts because there was no need to build a dome. Do you agree with that?

Caroline Um ... no. I think it'll help a lot. Definitely. The construction costs aren't difficult to calculate. The difficult question is, what sort of people will visit the dome? I'm sure it'll be popular with families with young children, for example. So the project'll be good for getting information about the market.

Interviewer Do you think someone will build another dome like this somewhere, one day?

Caroline It's possible, yeah. Maybe there's a huge market for them. I mean, it's not a completely new idea. There's already a dome like this one in Japan.

▶▶ **38**

Interviewer Do you think we'll see a space tourism industry in the next ... five years? Is that realistic?

Caroline I think so, yeah. I'm not sure how big it'll be. It all depends how much it costs. You know, if a flight costs ... under fifty thousand dollars, I think there'll be a lot of demand. If tickets cost over five hundred thousand dollars, very few people will buy them. Obviously, it'll be expensive. The question is, how expensive?

Interviewer Some people say two hundred thousand dollars is a realistic price.

Caroline Mmm ... well, that's probably about right for a short-term objective. In the long-term, I think the cost will need to be less than that. Probably less than half that.

Interviewer What do think space tourists will want? What sort of experience?

Caroline Um ... I think they'll want ... I think it has to be a real space trip. If it's too short, then people won't be happy. I don't think it needs to last for hours, but a couple of minutes won't be enough. It has to be worth the money.

Interviewer What do you think it will take to really make space tourism take off?

Caroline If somebody shows that it's possible, for a reasonable price, I think that'll be the start. If the first company is successful, a lot of others will follow. And, obviously, the top priority is safety. That's the big challenge – to show that it's safe.

▶▶ **39**

Assistant GlenAir, good afternoon. How can I help you?

Customer Hello. I'd like to fly to Lisbon at the end of May.

Assistant Lisbon?

Customer Yes.

Assistant What date are you planning to leave?

Customer On May the twenty-fourth.

Assistant May the twenty-fourth. Is it a return flight?

Customer A return, yes. I want to come back on the thirty-first.

Assistant The thirty-first of May ... OK, the cheapest fare's fifty-five pounds.

Customer That's for a return.

Assistant Yes.

Customer OK. Um ... and can I change the date if I need to?

Assistant No. For that fare, you can't change the booking, and there's no refund if you cancel.

Customer Right. So fifty-five pounds. And are there any extra charges? For airport tax, or ...

Assistant No, that's included.

Customer OK. Um ... oh, that's the other question – what's the maximum baggage allowance? Because I want to take a surfboard with me.

Assistant Right. Well, the maximum allowance is twenty kilograms. The excess baggage charge is six pounds per kilogram, but for a surfboard ...

▶▶ **40**

Customer ... OK, can I book a seat, then, please?

Assistant Yes. Can I take your name, please?

Customer Sure. It's Simon Brigton. B-R-I-G-T-O-N.

Assistant And Simon is S-I-M-O-N?

Customer That's right.

Assistant And how would you like to pay?

Customer Do you take Visa?

Assistant Of course, no problem. Could I take the number please?

Customer Sure, it's four six double seven, double three double four, two two two one, four double five. And the expiry date is August ... two thousand and nine.

Assistant Thank you. So, just to confirm, that's one ticket to Lisbon, flying out on May the twenty-fourth at six fifty and returning on May the thirty-first at seventeen thirty. The total cost is fifty-five pounds, including taxes.

Customer OK.

Assistant Check in opens two hours before take-off and closes half an hour before.

Customer OK. Just one more thing ... could I have an aisle seat?

Assistant You can choose your seat when you check in. Obviously, it's best to check in as early as possible.

Customer Right, OK.

Maria We use the same software – a system called Nurec – to control all the production processes.

Jerome Nurec?

Maria Yeah. Have you worked with it before?

Jerome No, I haven't used that one. I've used TP Control.

Maria Right. We used that here, a few years ago. So did you use TP in Cape Town?

Jerome Yeah. Then when I was in Boston, we used a system called Arrow.

Maria Oh, I've worked with that before.

Jerome We have so many different types of software in this company, it's unbelievable.

Maria I know. And we've changed so many times, as well. Have you ever used Conductor?

Jerome Conductor? No. I've never heard of it.

Maria That was the system they had when I joined. It was very good, actually.

Jerome That's the trouble, isn't it? These things change all the time, but do they really improve?

1 been   2 made   3 found   4 had   5 written   6 done   7 gone   8 flown   9 taken   10 sent   11 seen

Yves Yves Cordier.

Andy Yves, it's Andy Bell.

Yves Andy, hi. How are things?

Andy Going quite well.

Yves Is everything nearly ready?

Andy Well, we've got a full accounts department. I interviewed someone on Monday and she's accepted the post. Sara Bernard. I've already sent her details through to personnel, so that's gone well …

Yves OK, good. And what about the IT system? Have they installed that yet?

Andy Well, that's more difficult. Um … I've found two technicians so far, er, but unfortunately, I haven't found the third person we need, so …

Yves So you haven't finished the IT installation?

Andy No, we … we haven't actually started it yet. But …

Yves You haven't started it yet? Andy, we need to open that office in two weeks!

Andy I know. I've spoken to Daniela in the Zurich office and she's going to send someone next week. I think we can still open on time.

Yves We need to. How long is it going to take for you to get …

46

Brendan This is amazing – this article in the paper. Somebody's planning to do a parachute jump from space.

Lisa From *space*?

Brendan Yeah. An Australian. He's going to jump from a balloon, from forty thousand metres. So that's, what … forty kilometres.

Lisa That's pretty high. When I did my jump, it was from one thousand metres.

Brendan You've done a parachute jump?

Lisa Yeah.

Brendan Seriously?

Lisa Yeah!

47

Brendan You've done a parachute jump?

Lisa Yeah.

Brendan Seriously?

Lisa Yeah!

Brendan When?

Lisa About … four years ago. A group of us went, from my last company.

Brendan Wow! I'm impressed! So what was it like?

Lisa Fantastic! When you jump out of the plane, it's … it's just amazing.

Brendan You weren't too scared, then?

Lisa I was before I jumped. Everyone's frightened before their first jump. But as soon as your parachute opens, it's … it's actually quite relaxing. You're just there in the air – you've got this incredible view …

Brendan Yeah, I bet. And what about the landing?

Lisa It was OK. Not too hard.

Brendan Because that's the most dangerous moment, isn't it?

Lisa Well, yeah! Even if you jump without a parachute, it's not dangerous until you land!

Brendan No, good point!

Presenter It's been an excellent start to the year for Geo-Core. Your share price has risen by forty-two percent in the first quarter of this year. Not a bad performance – the S&P 500 has fallen by three percent so far this year.

Alan Yes. We're obviously very happy with the results we've had. Our profit has increased by twenty-six percent this quarter … which is better than we forecast – our forecast was for a twenty percent increase.

Presenter What's the main reason for that?

Alan I think, simply, it's because demand has been very strong. Our sales have been good. Um … the oil price has risen, um …

Presenter Obviously, your company doesn't sell oil – you're an exploration company, you work for oil companies and … and look for new oil reserves.

Alan That's right.

Presenter But what do high oil prices mean for your business?

Alan Well, prices are high because, basically, there isn't enough oil to meet demand. That means we need to find more ... which is our job, so ... rising oil prices are certainly good news for us ...

Presenter And looking to the future, do you think that ...

▶▶ **51**

Interviewer How important are property prices in the economy?

Roy In the UK, most people invest most of their money in their house. So property prices are extremely important.

Interviewer Mmm. What's your view on the UK property market? Do you think prices are too high?

Roy Well, in recent years, prices have gone up ... ten to twenty percent a year, um ... in some years even more. But inflation has been just two or three percent a year. So I think it's clear that, um ... the boom has to end.

Interviewer Mmm. The last property market crash, in the UK, was in the late 1980s, and it put the UK economy into a recession. Do you think the same thing will happen again?

Roy I don't think prices will crash. The ... the economic situation was different in the late 80s ... interest rates rose quite fast just before property prices fell. Today, the Bank of England is much more careful with ... with changes in interest rates. The other important difference, I think, is that then unemployment was quite high. Today, it's very low – about five percent. So the economic situation's completely different. So I don't think prices will crash, but it is possible they'll fall a little bit. Or stay at the same level for a few years.

Interviewer Banks have lent people a lot of money in recent years. People have got big mortgages. Do you think that'll be a problem? Will people have less money to spend in the future?

Roy Oh, certainly. Because the loans haven't just been mortgages – people have also borrowed money to spend in the shops. So far, that's helped the economy, because spending has been high. But at the end of the day, people will have to pay the money back. So I think we'll see lower consumer spending over the next few years.

▶▶ **52**

Valerie So, is your hotel OK? Did you sleep well?

Naomi Yes, fine thanks. I watched TV for a while, then had an early night. I watched a bit of that ... quiz show ... *Who Wants To Be A Millionaire?* – the French version.

Valerie Ah, really?

Naomi It's exactly the same as in the UK. The studio, the music ...

Valerie Yes, I think a lot of those kinds of shows are the same.

Naomi Do you have *The Weakest Link*? It's a quiz show, and the presenter's really horrible to the contestants.

Valerie Oh, yes. Yes, it's the same in France. I've seen the English version, as well, on satellite TV.

Naomi And do you have programmes like *Big Brother*? You know, with people living in a house, and there are cameras filming all the time.

Valerie Yes, we had a similar thing a few years ago. Do you have that programme, um ... in France it's called *Star Academy* ... er, with people who want to be pop stars, and, er, people vote, um ...

Naomi Yeah. It's called *Fame Academy* in England. There've been so many things like that on television in the last few years. Reality TV.

Valerie Reality TV, yeah. It's been the same in France. At home, I have satellite TV, and I get English programmes ...

▶▶ **53**

Valerie At home, I have satellite TV, and I get English programmes on BBC Prime. They show things like quiz shows, documentaries, comedy programmes. I find comedies quite difficult to understand.

Naomi Yeah, I bet.

Valerie There's a talk show, as well, where they interview famous people. I think the presenter's very well known in Britain. His name's um ... oh ...

Naomi Michael Parkinson?

Valerie Yes! They also show some good children's programmes. My little boy watches *Teletubbies*.

Naomi Oh yeah.

Valerie There's another thing I sometimes watch. What's the name for the type of programme ... it's about, not real people, they're actors, but about ... just everyday life in a street or, um ...

Naomi A soap opera. Or a soap.

Valerie That's it!

Valerie There's a soap about the people who live in a ... a square in London. I ... I can't remember ...

Naomi Not *EastEnders*?

Valerie *EastEnders*. That's it. What's so funny?

Naomi Valerie, I can't believe you watch *EastEnders* ... in Paris!

Valerie Actually, I'd like to watch more films in English. On French TV, when they show American films, the voices are in French. How do you say that? They're ...

Naomi Dubbed.

Valerie Dubbed?

Naomi Yeah.

Valerie They're nearly always dubbed in French. On some channels, they show the original film with ... you know, text at the bottom of the screen with, er ... with the translation.

Naomi With subtitles?

Valerie Subtitles, yeah. But I don't like that because you read but you don't really listen to ...

So, first, let's look at our present advertising strategy. How are we promoting the brand at the moment? As you know, we advertise in the press – most of our press ads are in magazines read by the eighteen to twenty-four age group. We also use adverts on billboards. We occasionally use TV commercials. And, of course, we market the brand with sponsorship in sports – we sponsor basketball, snowboarding and surfing.

At the moment, our spending on advertising is high as a percentage of sales. The reason for that is the cost of TV commercials. But the problem is, to make TV commercials work, you need a lot of them. A lot more than we have at present. Now, obviously we don't have the budget for that. So, in my opinion, TV commercials are not the right strategy for Sway.

But that doesn't mean we can't advertise on TV. We can. The way to do it more cheaply is to use product placement. The way product placement works is …

Colleague	So, the products are seen in films and TV programmes. They're just … *seen* on a table or …
Amy	That's right. Or in our case, with clothes, they're worn by an actor, um …
Colleague	And you see the logo.
Amy	Sometimes, yeah. It depends. You can't always … control what happens. Often, products are given to the film company for free. So you know an actor is going to … to wear your jacket, for example, but … you don't know if you'll actually see the logo.
Colleague	So you can't say to the film company, we want to … see this part of the jacket, or …
Amy	Well, you can, but then, usually, you have to pay. Sometimes, the film company is paid by the advertiser. And then you have more control. I mean … sometimes, the name of a product is said by an actor. But that's … in a film – you're talking big money for that sort of thing.
Colleague	Yeah, I bet. … And when did companies start doing this? I guess it's done more now than in the past.
Amy	I think the first placements were used in films in the 1960s, for cigarettes. But the big business really started in the 80s. I think the best placement, though, was, um … did you see *Forrest Gump*? The Apple placement was done very well in that.
Colleague	For Apple computers?
Amy	Yeah. There's a scene where Forrest Gump gets a letter from Apple …

Tony	The business has done well over the last three years. And I think now's the right time to expand – to open a new office, hire some good people … hire a manager to help me, and … you know, become a bigger organisation. So I need to raise finance, and to do that, I'd like to try and find some people who want to buy shares in the company.
Jane	Right. So you're not planning to borrow the money?
Tony	No. And to expand quickly, I need more than just money. I need your advice on how to manage the expansion.
Jane	OK. Well, you're certainly right to recruit a manager for the new office. I'm sure you know what it's like to work hard, seven days a week … Obviously, you're an entrepreneur, you set up the company. But as the organisation grows, each year, your job changes gradually. If you open a new office, obviously that's a big change, so your job needs to change significantly.
Tony	Sure.
Jane	Have you thought about your future with the company?
Tony	… You mean, do I want to sell the whole business?
Jane	No, that's not what I mean. It's just that, if I find you some investors, they'll want some management control. It won't really be *your* business any more. You understand what I'm getting …
Tony	Sure, sure.
Jane	It's not a decision you can make easily. But you need to think about your future carefully.

1   I think the best thing about the Internet is … the fact that you can find information so easily. You know, you type a keyword into a search engine, and you get a huge list of websites. The worst thing is the problem of viruses. You certainly need antivirus software. And you've got to keep it up-to-date as well – keep downloading and installing updates. But, it's not too much trouble to find a …

2   It's good that you can manage your bank accounts via the Internet. That saves a lot of time. Once you've registered you just … put in your password, log in and … you've got access to all your accounts and everything … from home. It's um …. it's good. I think it took a long time before people were confident with, um … secure servers, with the security side of it, but now it's … it's just part of everyday life. It's like paying by credit card online …

3   I'm a member of an investment website, which is part of a magazine. I pay ten pounds a month and I get access to articles from the current issue and I can search for articles from previous issues as well. They show current share prices, so you can follow your portfolio. Each time you just log in, with a user name and a password and it automatically lists your shares, shows the current price …

▶▶ 61

A OK, so our objective is to think of some new ideas. How could we make the product better? What areas of the product could we improve? Any suggestions?

B What about changing the packaging? We could change the material.

A Yeah. Packaging material. OK.

C How about changing the size?

A Of the CD?

C No, the pack. Why don't we sell more CDs in a pack, for example?

A OK. Yeah. So, bigger packs. They could be smaller, as well.

B Why not sell big boxes – big storage boxes, with lots of CDs in them? Then you wouldn't need packaging.

A So that would be a new product. A storage box.

C We could sell CDs with numbers printed on them – say from one to a hundred. Then you wouldn't need to write on the CD. You could make a note of what was on each CD number, and then find it easily. So we could sell, say, packs of ten. So you would have one to ten, or eleven to twenty, and so on.

B That's a good idea. We could use that idea with the storage box. So we could produce a big plastic box with, say, a hundred blank CDs in it, with the CDs numbered one to a hundred.

A Mmm, that's a, that's an interesting idea.

▶▶ 64

Interviewer People often say that some nationalities are more polite than others. Do you think that's true? And do you think you have to be more or less polite when you work with people from different cultures?

Sandra You don't have to be more or less *polite*. I think it's more a question of how *direct* people are. You should always be polite. It's just that, in some cultures, it's OK to be direct, and in others, um … it's not. For example, in Germany, in business, it's best to be very direct. Generally, people ask direct questions and … they like direct answers.

Interviewer But in the UK, generally, people are less direct, aren't they?

Sandra Well, they're not afraid to say they disagree or … or to criticise suggestions. You don't have to say you agree all the time. But … you know, people say things like, '*I'm not sure* I agree.', or … '*Maybe* it would be better to do it another way'. I've always found, in different cultures, the best way to disagree or … or criticise ideas is to make it clear you're criticising the *suggestion* – you shouldn't criticise the *person*.

Interviewer In Japan, it's *very* important not to criticise people, isn't it?

Sandra Yes. You should never criticise anyone directly. It's … for the Japanese, it's very impolite. That's why, often, in companies in Japan, people have to make decisions in groups. Everyone has to agree.

Interviewer So what's your general advice? Do you think people should change the way they communicate in different cultures or … or should you just be yourself?

Sandra I think you should always be yourself, um … but I think, to be successful, you need to change *how* you say things.

▶▶ 66

1 One suggestion is, we could close the old plant and move everything to a new site. I think we should consider that option. It's a possibility.

2 There would be a lot of benefits if we had just one plant. It would be better, um … it would be easier to manage supplies and deliveries. Energy costs would be another advantage.

3 We know how much we would save if we had a new production line. We've all read the report and seen the figures for that. And from the forecasts we know more or less …

4 I think one large plant looks like a good option. That's my first impression.

5 OK, shall we sum up, then? I think we've made quite good progress. We've got quite a long list of ideas. I think we should just consider two or three proposals. So let's look at the list …

6 **A** I don't think it would be a good idea to spend so much. I'm worried about the economic situation. I think it's too uncertain.

   B So what would you recommend?

   C Let's just talk about disadvantages for the moment.

   B I just wouldn't recommend such a big investment. We have to be careful.

▶▶ 68

Assistant Hello.

Rachel Hello. I've just missed my connection to London. I was booked on the nine thirty. I just want to check if my ticket's valid for the next train … at half past ten.

Assistant Um … ah yes, you're OK. Obviously, you won't have a seat reservation.

Rachel No. Is it too late to make one?

Assistant Mmm, I'm afraid so.

Rachel Will it be busy?

Assistant It's usually quite busy, yeah. You'll probably get a seat in first class, if you want to change your ticket.

Rachel Would I have to cancel this ticket? Would I get a refund, or …?

Assistant	You can just upgrade it. You just pay a supplement. I can check how much it would cost.
Rachel	Um … oh, no, it's OK. I don't think my company would pay my expenses in first class!
Assistant	Ah.
Rachel	OK, thanks. Oh … is the ten thirty on time, by the way?
Assistant	Um … It's running four minutes late.
Rachel	OK, thanks.

▶▶ 70

1 **A** I'm afraid your ticket's not valid on this train.
   B Isn't it? I thought I could use it on any train.
   A No. It's only valid on trains leaving after ten am.
   B Oh. I didn't realise.
   A The fare's a bit higher on the earlier trains. It's not a big difference.
   B OK. So can I just pay the extra?
   A Yes. I'll just check how much it is.

2 We regret to inform passengers that flight TL seven four nine to Geneva has been cancelled due to a technical problem. Flight TL seven four nine to Geneva is cancelled. Passengers for this flight should check in at gate nine D and await a transfer to the next flight to Zurich.

3 **A** Good morning.
   B Morning. I checked in yesterday evening. My room's booked for a second night, for tonight, but I need to stay in town a third night, um … tomorrow night – I've got another meeting which wasn't planned. Could I book my room for an extra night?
   A Hmm. I'm afraid we're full tomorrow night, um … Just a moment. I'll see if there's a room free at our other hotel. It's just a few minutes walk from here. If that's …
   B Yeah, that's fine.
   A Hello Paul, it's Alex. Have you got a single room free tomorrow night? OK, great. Can you hold it for me? I'll phone you back with the details. Thanks. … OK. That's booked.
   B Excellent.

▶▶ 71

A key question, when you start to design a high-speed train is, how wide is the track? What's the distance between the rails? Because the width of the track doesn't just give you the width of the train. The height of the train is also limited by the width of the track. Obviously, trains have to be stable, especially if they have to go round curves quite fast. Tall, narrow designs are unstable. So, for better stability, a wide track is better.

The trouble with standard tracks is, they're quite narrow. For high-speed trains, this is a problem if there are a lot of curves in the line. Now, you can limit the problem. To help the train stay on the track, you make it quite heavy … and you put most of the weight as low as possible, below the floor. Now of course, a design that's very heavy isn't very efficient. Just look at the big, thick pieces of steel used in trains, um … to get an idea of how much weight there is. So it's very inefficient. And another problem, of course, that you have to deal with is …

▶▶ 74

Dennis	OK. Let's make a list of dangers on the tarmac … and then we can make a list of safety precautions to help prevent accidents. So, first of all, what are the main hazards? Any suggestions?
Woman	Planes, when they're moving.
Dennis	OK … Moving planes.
Man	Noise from engines … from the jets. You need to wear ear protection.
Dennis	Uhuh, OK. Noise … ear protection.
Woman	Other vehicles, moving around.
Dennis	OK, good. Moving vehicles. They are the biggest hazard on the tarmac. Not planes, but vehicles: buses, trucks, cars … . What precautions can you take to help avoid accidents – to prevent ground vehicles hitting people?
Woman	Er, everyone should wear a green jacket.
Dennis	OK. High visibility clothing. Essential. Does anyone know why moving vehicles are especially dangerous at airports?
Woman	Because they drive around quite fast?
Dennis	They often do, yeah. They're not allowed to, though. The health and safety regulations say that every employee is responsible for the safety of others. But there's another reason why moving vehicles are particularly hazardous at airports. Any other ideas?
Man	Because you can't hear them, because of all the noise … from jets and, um …
Dennis	Exactly. If you're standing near a plane with its engines running, you can't always hear vehicles coming. Just now, someone said you need to wear ear protection. For some jobs – for example, if you have to stand in front of moving planes to guide the pilots, then, yes, you need to protect your ears. But only *some* people need ear protection, *some* of the time.
Woman	So how do we know if we need ear protection or not? Are there standard procedures?
Dennis	Yes. We'll look at those a bit later on …

▶▶ 75

Interviewer	A lot of people have to think about safety regulations in their jobs. But for pilots, safety is *extremely* important, isn't it?
Mike	Absolutely. It's all about procedures, in fact. Pilots must know exactly what to do in all situations.
Interviewer	Obviously you need a lot of experience.

Mike	Yes ... to get an airline pilot's licence you need a minimum number of hours flying time. You must have at least one thousand five hundred hours. And you must be at least twenty-three years old. Obviously, most professional pilots are a lot older than that.
Interviewer	Sure. And do all pilots have to be able to speak English? Is that a requirement?
Mike	Yes – to fly internationally.
Interviewer	What are the main safety procedures you have to follow? Are there certain things that are especially important?
Mike	We have a lot of checklists. There are things you must always check before each flight. You mustn't take off until you've checked everything. The first thing is, you walk around the plane, outside, and check that ... you know, nothing's broken or ... cracked.
Interviewer	That there are no cracks in the wings!
Mike	Actually, most planes have cracks in their wings! Very, very small ones. It's perfectly safe.
Interviewer	Right! And apparently, you can still land if an engine breaks down, can't you?
Mike	You can *take off* if an engine breaks down. If it happens a few seconds before take-off, um ... if you're above a certain speed, the procedure is, you mustn't try to stop, because the runway isn't long enough. So you take off, fly around the airport, and then land again.

▶▶ 76

1

Assistant	Hello.
Woman	Hello. I'd like some information about the gym.
Assistant	The health and fitness club?
Woman	Yes. Is it open to everyone? Can anyone go in?
Assistant	Yes, sure.
Woman	And is that where the sauna is?
Assistant	There is a sauna in the health and fitness club, yes. There's another on Deck C, next to the swimming pool, as well.
Woman	OK. ... OK, thanks very much.
Assistant	You're welcome.

2

Man	Hi.
Assistant	Good morning.
Man	I think there's a problem with the TV in my room. I can't switch it on for some reason.
Assistant	Have you put the card in?
Man	The card? ... I didn't see a card with it, um ...
Assistant	Right. You need a card. There's a small charge if you want TV. It's eighteen dollars for the full ten-day cruise.

Man	Eighteen dollars?
Assistant	Yes. You just need to sign a form, then we give you a card, and you put it in the TV. You get all the major satellite channels sir ...

3

Woman	Excuse me, I've just read the poster, over there, about the show in the, um ... Laguna bar tomorrow night. It says you need to book. Are there any tickets left?
Assistant	Yes.
Woman	OK. And how much are they?
Assistant	They're free. It's just it's usually quite popular, so we prefer to issue tickets, then people aren't disappointed if they don't get a seat.
Woman	Right. OK, so can I book two seats, please?
Assistant	Sure. Can I take your room number?

▶▶ 78

Victoria	OK. Shall we make a start? ... Er, just to say, John Gates can't make it. He sends his apologies. He's had to go to an urgent meeting with a customer. John's asked me to chair the meeting ... so I'm in the hot seat! OK, first, has everyone got an agenda? John told me copies were circulated on Monday.
George	I got the agenda, but I didn't get a copy of the minutes from the meeting last week.
Victoria	... The meeting last week?
George	John told me you all met last week, to talk about the conference. I didn't attend. I wasn't here last week, so I don't know what ...
Victoria	Oh, that. No, we didn't hold a meeting. We didn't take minutes or anything, it was just ... some of us had a talk, during a coffee break ...
George	Oh, OK.
Victoria	Don't worry, you didn't miss anything. So, we've called this meeting to talk about the sales conference next January. We need to look at the programme ... to plan what we're going to do ... during the two days. So let's look at the first item on the agenda, then: the main theme for the conference. As you know, each year we have a theme ...

▶▶ 80

a

Amelia	I can speak to Sam Wu, in Beijing, and see if he can give a talk about Chinese culture. I can contact Mai Cheng, as well.
Victoria	OK, great.
Amelia	I'll call them as soon as we finish.

b

George	So before we decide, I'll visit all three hotels. And we definitely don't want to use the conference centre we used last time.
Amelia	No. I think everyone agreed that it wasn't ...

c

George So we're saying the last week in January. But, um ... we won't book until we get replies from the branches.

Victoria No. I think we need to ask everyone just to be sure.

d

Amelia Just before we finish, there's just one thing, that's not on the agenda. Tom Watts emailed me to say he wants to ... organise some gifts, for everyone who attends.

Victoria What sort of gifts?

Amelia I don't know. He didn't say. I'll ask him when I speak to him tomorrow. I need to phone him.

▶▶ 82

George Hello.

Victoria Hello George, it's Victoria. How are you?

George Not too bad.

Victoria I'm just calling about the quotes, from the three hotels, for the conference. Have you got copies of all of them?

George Um ... yes. Yeah, they're here on my, er, desk ... somewhere.

Victoria Could you email them to me?

George Um ... I can fax them. I've only got hard copies – I haven't got the files in the computer, so, um ...

Victoria OK, fine.

George I've got to go to a meeting in about a quarter of an hour, so ... I'll send them now.

Victoria Yeah, OK. There's no rush. This afternoon's fine, if, um ...

George No, no, it's no problem. I'll send them now.

Victoria OK, great. Then maybe we can discuss them later today?

George Sure. I'll be in the office all afternoon.

Victoria OK. I'll call you later this afternoon, then.

George OK.

▶▶ 83

Victoria So I've looked at the three quotes, from all three hotels. And, obviously, we've visited all three as well. Um ... and I think the best place is the Darley.

George Yeah. I agree. The trouble is, it's the most expensive.

Victoria Yeah. Their price is, what, ten percent higher than the other two.

George Hmm. It *is* their first offer, though. I haven't negotiated with them yet.

Victoria No. Could you try to get a better price from them?

George I can try, yeah. I'll call the manager in the morning. Um ... what's her name ... Heidi Wells.

Victoria Tell her you've spoken to your boss, and er ... tell her I said they can have the contract if they can give us a ten percent discount.

George And why don't I show her the offers from the other hotels? I can go and see her, and take the quotes with me. That's probably better than phoning.

Victoria Yeah, OK.

George And what if she says they can't give us ten percent, but they can give ... I don't know, five percent?

Victoria Well, do your best to get ten percent. If she offers you ... five percent, or whatever, then ... tell her you'll have to speak to me again. Tell her you can accept ten percent immediately, but, if not, you'll have to get back to me.

George OK, fine. I'll phone her now and see if I can arrange a meeting tomorrow.

Victoria Right. I'll give John Gates a call and give him an update – tell him what our strategy is!

George So I'll give you a call, um ... after I've met Heidi Wells, tomorrow.

Victoria Right. OK, well good luck!

George Thanks. Bye.

▶▶ 84

1

Amelia Hi Tom.

Tom Hi, Amelia. How are you?

Amelia Very well, thanks. How are you?

Tom Fine, thank you. Sorry I'm late.

Amelia That's OK.

Tom My train was delayed.

Amelia Oh, the trains here are never on time ...

2

Tom Hello.

Receptionist Hello.

Tom I've come for a meeting with Amelia Donovan. My name's Tom Watts. I'm afraid I'm a little bit late.

Receptionist I'll give her a call ... Amelia, Tom Watts is in reception ... OK. She'll be with you in a moment. If you'd like to have a seat.

Tom Thanks.

3

Tom We've made good progress there.

Amelia Yeah. We're about halfway through the agenda.

Tom It's quite hot in here. Do you mind if I open the window?

Amelia No, not at all. Shall we take a break?

Tom Yes, good idea.

Amelia We can go out and get some fresh air, if you like. We can walk across to the cafeteria and get a coffee over there ...

4

Amelia	OK. This is my office. After you.
Tom	Thank you.
Amelia	Shall I take your coat?
Tom	Yes, thank you ... Here you are.
Amelia	Thanks. Can I get you anything to drink? Coffee? Tea?
Tom	No, I'm fine thanks.
Amelia	We can start straight away, if you like. I'll give you a copy of ...

▶▶ **85**

Tom	It's a beautiful day.
Amelia	Yeah, it's been hot like this all week. It'll probably last until Friday, then rain all weekend!
Tom	Yeah.
Amelia	So how was your trip? You said your train was delayed?
Tom	Yeah. It left on time, but then we stopped at a station somewhere. They said we had to wait for another train coming ...

▶▶ **86**

Tom	Would you like a CC Software company lolly?
Amelia	A *what*?
Tom	A company lollipop. They're gifts ... for the conference.
Amelia	Oh, I see!
Tom	Here you are.
Amelia	Thanks. Company lollipops?
Tom	I give them to all my customers.
Amelia	Really?
Tom	Sure. ... They're quite popular in the States ... as business gifts.
Amelia	Oh, yes? So they're not your idea, then?
Tom	No. I just bought them.
Amelia	Oh, right. They're in the company colours. ... So, what flavour are they?

Acknowledgements

The authors would like to acknowledge above all the significant contribution to the course made by Nathalie and Aimy Ibbotson, and Evgenia Miassoedova. They were a constant source of support and ideas at all stages of the project and displayed remarkable patience!

Thanks also to: Will Capel for believing in the project and for his advice and expertise during the critical early stages of development, Sally Searby for her encouragement and commitment to getting the best out of the course, Clare Abbott for her excellent editorial input – especially in guiding the material through key improvements to the concept and methodology, Elin Jones for her valuable editorial advice, ideas and positive support – much appreciated during the intense phase of writing the first level, and Chris Capper for his helpful input on the early units. A big thanks to our editor Nick Robinson, whose positive energy, ideas and feel for the material have been instrumental in shaping the second level. And a special thanks to our copy editor Fran Banks, for giving *Business Start-up* the benefit of her expertise, eagle eyes and extremely hard work.

We would also like to thank the many reviewers who have offered valuable comments on the material at various stages of development, including Alex Case, Helen Forrest, Radoslaw Lewandowski, Rosemary Richey and Robert Szulc.

The publisher would like to thank the following for permission to reproduce photographs:

© Suzy Bennett/Alamy: p. 54*mr*, © Mark Boulton/Alamy: p. 86*br*, © William Eckersley/Alamy: pp. 34-35, © Imagestate/Alamy: p. 16*br*, © Jeff Morgan/Alamy: p. 50, ©The Photolibrary Wales/Alamy: p. 68, © Pictorial Press/Alamy: p. 54*b*, © Popperphoto/Alamy: p. 24*l*, © Stockdisc Premium/Alamy: p. 17, © Paul Springett/Alamy: p. 86*bl*, © A.T.Willett/Alamy: p. 24*r*; Martin Barlow, photographersdirect.com: p. 40; Caryn Becker, photographersdirect.com: p. 20*tl*; Bjorn Beheydt, photographersdirect.com: p. 9*mr*; © Bettmann/CORBIS: p. 60*tm* & *tr*, © Chris Carroll/CORBIS: p. 6*tr*, © Walter Hodges/CORBIS: p. 79*t*, © Louie Psihoyos/CORBIS: pp. 26-27, © Jim Sugar/CORBIS: p. 20*bl*; Edifice/Gillian Darley, photographersdirect.com: p. 12*l*; © EMPICS: pp. 16*tr, mr* & *bl*, 54*tl*, 66*r*; Getty Images: pp. 9*(d)*, 14 *(all)*, 16*tl* & *c*, 18, 23, 25, 37, 38, 39, 46-47, 48, 54*tr*, 60*tl*, 61, 62, 63, 64, 69, 70-71; Erik Daniels/Imagestate: p. 21, Premium Stock/Imagestate: p. 43; www.istockphoto.com: pp. 33, 79*b*, 86*tl, tm* & *tr*; Bob Lendrum, photographersdirect.com: p. 58; www.davidlevenson.com: p. 56*l*; www.lyonsanddebono.com: p. 60*b*; www.mclaren.com: p. 20*(c)*; Photolibrary: p. 57; Sergio Piumatti, photographersdirect.com: p. 54*ml*; Rex Features: p. 16*tm*; Superstock: p. 12*r*; Topfoto *(Darley Hotel is a fictitious name)*: p. 75; Transrapid International GmbH & Co. KG: p. 66*l*; Photos courtesy of Vekoma Rides Manufacturing. B.V. – The Netherlands: p. 9*t, bl* & *br*; Zefa Visual Media: p. 24.

The author and publishers are grateful to the authors, publishers and others who have given permission for the use of copyright material identified in the text. It has not always been possible to identify the source of material used or to contact the copyright holders and in such cases the publishers would welcome information from the copyright owners.

For the text and photos on p. 8: International Association of Amusement Parks and Attractions (IAAPA); for the text and photos on p. 9: from www.vekoma.com, with permission of Vekoma Rides Manufacturing B.V; for the photos on p. 20: from BBC Motion Gallery, reproduced with permission of BBC Worldwide Ltd; for the text and photos on p. 22: Vladi Private Islands GMBH (www.vladi.de); for the text on pp. 26-27: adapted from www.bbc.co.uk/dinosaurs website, reproduced with permission of BBC Worldwide Ltd; for the text and images on p. 31: from www.ssfconf.com, reproduced with permission of South San Francisco Conference Center Authority; for the text and photos on pp. 36-37: from www.my-tropical-islands.com, reproduced by permission of Tropical Island Management GmbH; for the text on pp. 38-39: from www.virgin.com, with permission of Virgin Galactic; for the text on pp. 46-47: from www.stevefossett.com, with permission of Marathon Racing Inc; for the chart and graph on p. 50: from *The Economist* (www.economist.com), © The Economist Newspaper Limited, London, 2002 and 2004; for the text and image on p. 52: from 'Who Wants To Be A Millionaire', with permission of Celador International Ltd; for the Apple logo on p. 55: reproduced with permission of Apple Computer, Inc; for the 'boo hoo' jacket cover on p. 56: reproduced with permission of The Random House Group; for the text and photo on p. 77: from www.lindaslollies.com, with permission of Linda's Lollies Co, Inc.

Commissioned Photography by Gareth Boden p.6*l, rm* & *rb*, p. 11, 30, 32, 72, 76, 77*lm*

Cover images by (the graph) Alamy; (the runner) Getty

Picture Research by Sandie Huskinson-Rolfe of PHOTOSEEKERS

Book design by Pentacor**big**